LITTLE BOOK OF
BURGHLEY

LITTLE BOOK OF
BURGHLEY

First published in the UK in 2013

© G2 Entertainment Limited 2013

www.G2ent.co.uk

Printed and bound in Europe

ISBN 978-1-782812-03-6

Contents

Introduction

Far Right: *Aerial view of the horse trials site, showing the magnitude of the event*

The sport of eventing in Britain is synonymous with the great country houses and their rolling parklands. Burghley Horse Trials, more than any other, epitomises the dream, its early September date casting an evocative late summer light over the mature trees, lush turf, peacefully grazing herd of fallow deer and golden-hued Barnack rag stone of one of England's finest Elizabethan houses which form the backdrop to the second oldest, continually running international three-day event in the world.

Burghley, which overlooks the pretty Lincolnshire market town of Stamford, has as its southern boundary Ermine Street, the old Roman road which ran from London to York. The house was built by William Cecil, a politician who served through turbulent times under Henry Vlll, Edward Vl and Elizabeth l, who appointed him Lord High Treasurer. In 1552 he inherited from his father the manor of 'Burleigh' and set about redesigning the original building. During the Civil War, the south front was bombarded by Cromwell's army.

The house, with its fairytale turreted roofs, owes much of its splendid baroque style and treasures to John Cecil, 5th Earl of Exeter who was married to a daughter of the 3rd Earl of Devonshire; the couple accrued many works of art during their Grand Tour of Europe, although they eventually died in debt a

a result of their lavish spending on art.

The 9th Earl (1725-93) extended the art collections, completed work on the state rooms and brought in the acclaimed landscape architect 'Capability' Brown. He gives his name to the landscaped gully and driveway which is part of the cross-country course today and still known as 'Capability's Cutting'. He also designed the three-arched Lion Bridge, another feature on the course, the lake, the orangery and the stables. These are not much used now – the stabling for the horse trials is temporary – apart from for Pony Club camps, but in 1971 Princess Anne's horse, Doublet, was billeted there.

The 10th Earl was bestowed the title of Marquess in 1801 for his charitable works. However, he had spent several years lying low in Shropshire in order to avoid his creditors under the cover of being a landscape painter. The romance with his second wife, Sarah Hoggins, is told in the Tennyson poem, *The Lord of Burghley*.

Early equestrian activity at Burghley centred around racing – there was a racecourse at Stamford, which eventually fell into disrepair – and hunting. The Burghley Hunt, formed

Left: Capability Brown's Lion Bridge, with Burghley's fairytale turrets in the background. The rider is Ireland's Geoff Curran on Shanaclough Crecora

INTRODUCTION

Far Right:
Philip Herbert, Burghley's clerk of the course

in the early 1900s as a pack of harriers, was dispersed during World War ll, re-started by the 6th Marquess and eventually disbanded in 1967. When the event started, it was traditional for competitors to go cub-hunting on the Saturday morning with Lord Burghley's hounds.

It is the 6th Marquess to whom we owe Burghley Horse Trials. A talented sportsman, he won an Olympic gold medal in the 400m hurdles in 1928 at the Amsterdam Games and a silver in the 400m relay in Los Angeles; he was famously played by Nigel Havers in the film *Chariots of Fire*.

At the time Burghley Horse Trials came into being, the world's two most important three-day events were Badminton, started by the Duke of Beaufort in 1949 to enable British riders to prepare for the Olympics, and Harewood in Yorkshire which was the big autumn event in the 1950s. The latter was blighted by foot-and-mouth disease in 1961 – it never ran again - and the Marquess enthusiastically invited the British Horse Society to transfer the event to Burghley, providing significant financial support to those early years.

Burghley Horse Trials is still committee-run and the office, within the park, is on the spot of the original somewhat basic 1961 'hut'. The estate is run by the Burghley House Preservation Trust; after Lord Exeter's death in 1981, the title passed to his brother, Martin, but he wanted to remain on his ranch in Canada, so Lord Exeter's daughter, Victoria Leatham, who was a director of Sotheby's and a regular on *Antiques Road Show*, became, with her husband Simon, custodian of Burghley and president of the Horse Trials.

Now Burghley is an all-woman affair with Victoria's daughter Miranda Rock as chairman of the trustees and Elizabeth Inman, who has worked there for more than 30 years, as horse trials director. A woman has yet to be appointed course-designer, however: in another circle, so typical of the sport, Capt Mark Phillips who as a rider won Burghley in 1973 and came agonisingly close to taking the world title in 1974, has that role.

Burghley has grown into one of the world's great sporting events; spectator numbers have increased from around 8,000 in those early days to about 150,000 and the plethora of high-quality tradestands has turned it into a major Christmas-shopping festival. Cross country day, with around 100,000 spectators, is one of the best-attended day's sport in the world – more than the Grand National or the FA Cup Final – and Burghley's takings help underpin financially the national sport of eventing in Britain.

Although Burghley and Badminton are technically the same level of difficulty, Burghley was always considered a stepping stone to Badminton for horses. Nowadays it is fair to say that Burghley is considered to be of top-flight difficulty, partly because its undulating terrain contrasts with Badminton's flat parkland, and some riders have described it as the 'toughest course in the world'.

Whereas Badminton is still very much a team selection trial for championships, Burghley is an arguably less pressurised, if no less competitive, occasion. Its combination of a relaxed ambience and top sporting occasion, organised by a knowledgeable team which leaves no stone unturned in its quest to provide the very best for horses, riders, owners and spectators, means Burghley is held in great affection by competitors who regularly vote it the best event in the world.

BURGHLEY EXPLAINED

Classification: Burghley Horse Trials is classified as a CCI★★★★ (CCI means *concours complet international*) by the sport's ruling body, the FEI (Federation Equestre Internationale), which is based in Lausanne, Switzerland. It is ranked 4-star (the level of most difficulty). For many years, Burghley and Badminton were the only 4-star events in the world, and they still attract the largest entry lists, but now there are four others: Kentucky (USA), Luhmühlen (Germany), Pau (France) and Adelaide (Australia).

The term horse trials to describe the sport has generally given way to the modern international term 'eventing' (it used to be known as 'combined training', a term the Americans still sometimes use, and across much of Continental Europe 'the military'). The term eventing stems from the sport being divided into 'one-day events' and 'three-day events', rather in the way that cricket has one-day internationals and five-day Test matches. However, somewhat confusingly, most three-day events, including Burghley, actually run over four days because it wouldn't be possible to accommodate all

Left: Lady Victoria Leatham is presented with a framed picture on her retirement as president of Burghley Horse Trials. Pictured with husband Simon, Liz Inman, Chairman Malcolm Wallace, and retired director, Bill Henson

the dressage into one day. Burghley's usual date is the first weekend in September.

Prizes: First prize at Burghley in 2013 is £60,000, with prize money down to 20th place. Burghley is also part of the Rolex Grand Slam, a rider challenge which links Kentucky, Badminton and Burghley and is worth $350,000 to the rider who can win all three in succession. For 2012 and 2013, Burghley was the finale of the HSBC FEI Classics™ series, which links all six CCI4★s and gives $150,000 to the rider who gains the most points across the six events.

Administration: Burghley Horse Trials is an event owned by the Burghley Trust. The President of the committee is Miranda Rock, Burghley's present head of trustees, the chairman is Richard Jewson and the event director is Elizabeth Inman. It is run from a permanent office on the estate. Land Rover became title sponsor in 2005.

FORMAT

The competition is divided into three phases (dressage, cross-country and show jumping); riders carry scores throughout and the lowest score wins. Nowadays, horse and rider have to be qualified to enter Burghley by achieving certain standards at previous international competitions.

In the **dressage** phase, horse and rider perform a pre-set test of linked movements, at walk, trot and canter, in an arena. Each movement is marked out of 10. The partnership is also judged on impulsion, submission, paces and rider. It is judged subjectively, by three judges (known as the ground jury), whose marks are averaged out to give a final score. The rider with the lowest mark at this stage is in the lead.

The **cross-country** phase is the sport's crowning glory and its pivot: a test of courage, fitness and communication between horse and rider, who negotiate a course of obstacles against the clock. At Burghley, the cross-country is about four miles long with around 30 separate solid fences, some of which may involve two, three or four jumping efforts or 'elements'. Riders earn 0.4 of a penalty for each second accrued over the optimum time. A refusal carries 20 penalties; a second refusal at the same fence is 40 penalties. The accumulation of three refusals on the course equals elimination from the competition, as does a fall.

The final **jumping** phase in eventing

Right: *Miranda Rock, president of the horse trials, and her husband Orlando*

is nothing like as big as the courses found in the top levels of the sport of pure show jumping. This is because the idea is for a horse to prove its fitness to jump after the galloping exertions of the day before and for the rider to prove that they can show judgement in producing a horse fit enough to complete three different phases. The jumping is, however, an exacting accuracy test which often produces nail-biting finales; competitors can see major prizes disappear in seconds if their horse hits a fence, while others can gain significant elevation from a clear round. Riders accrue four penalties per fence knocked down, plus four for a refusal and one per second after the time allowed is exceeded. Again, a fall equals elimination.

Horse inspections: The day before the competition starts, all the horses are trotted up in front of the ground jury and chief vet to establish their soundness and fitness to compete. The ground jury can eliminate a horse at this stage if it is lame or, if they are in any doubt, they can monitor the horse and eliminate it at a later stage in the competition. There is a second horse inspection on the final morning after cross-country and before show jumping, again to establish the horse's fitness to continue.

BURGHLEY RECORD-BREAKERS

• Sheila Willcox is the only rider to have won Badminton (1957, 1958, 1959), Burghley (1968) and Harewood (1956)

• Pippa Funnell is the only rider to have won Kentucky, Badminton and Burghley in succession, in the same 12 months (in 2003) to win the Rolex Grand Slam

• Ginny Elliot (nee Holgate, formerly Leng) is the only rider to have won Burghley four times in succession (1983-86); Mark Todd (1990-1991) and William Fox-Pitt (2007-08) have both won it twice in succession

• William Fox-Pitt holds the record for Burghley wins with six victories (1994, 2002, 2005, 2007, 2008, 2011); Mark Todd (1987, 1990, 1991, 1997, 1999) and Ginny Elliot (1983, 1984, 1985, 1986, 1989) have five wins apiece

• Andrew Nicholson has won three times (1995, 2000 and 2012)

• Dual winners are Lorna Clarke (neé Sutherland) in 1967 and 1978; Lucinda Prior-Palmer (now Green, 1977 and 1981); Richard Walker (1980 and 1982), Blyth Tait (1998 and 2001) and Andrew Hoy a remarkable 25 years apart in 1979 and 2004

• Only one horse has won Burghley twice: Priceless (under Ginny Leng) in 1983 and 1985

• The oldest equine winner is Lenamore, at the age of 17 in 2010, ridden by New Zealander Caroline Powell

• Only two mares have won Burghley: Maid Marion with Mark Phillips (1973) and Headley Britannia with Lucinda Fredericks (2006)

• British riders have won Burghley 34 times between 1961 and 2012; New Zealand riders won Burghley 11 times in the 25 years between 1987 and 2012; the other nations represented are Ireland, Argentina, USA (twice) and Australia (twice). No rider from continental Europe has won Burghley so far

The 1960s

At the time that Burghley began, horse trials was still very much a fledgling sport, in some respects unrecognisable against today's expectations of immaculate ground, percentages of clear cross-country rounds, computerisation, sponsor branding and health-and-safety. The 1961 season in Britain comprised 11 events, of which only a handful kept going over future decades, and the sport was, for most riders, only a small part of their equestrian lives.

Few riders 'specialised' as they do today. The most successful horse trials competitors were likely to have also competed in showing, hunter trials, showjumping, point-to-pointing, amateur racing, polo and, of course, they went hunting. Most participants were serving or former cavalry officers, very few made their living from horses – by instructing or dealing - and women were still barred from competing in Olympic Games.

There was still suspicion about the dressage phase, which was considered by many people to be both sissy and baffling. The first Burghley director, Brigadier James Grose, who was also director of the national umbrella body Horse Trials (now British Eventing), initially found it quite difficult to persuade people to be fence judges as they feared that the 'artificial' sport would lure people away from the hunting field. Now, the local hunting fraternity forms the mainstay of

the volunteer force, as they do at many horse trials, and the four sections of the course are still known as Burghley, Cottesmore, Fitzwilliam and Quorn.

The first members of the Burghley committee were Lord Exeter (president), Sir Henry Tate (vice-president), John Langton, the land agent at Burghley, and Giles Floyd, with James Grose and the cross-country course-designer, Bill Thomson, who is now remembered through a course-building bursary in his name.

Bill, who is considered one of the most influential figures in the development of the sport, was very

Right: *Glamour girl Sheila Willcox, the 1968 winner, pictured on her comeback from injury in 1964*

much the architect of the idea that cross-country courses should encourage, and not frighten, horses; he perpetuated the idea of having alternative routes at certain fences so that horses were not baulked, and his ambition was very much to see horses go on from Burghley to glory at Badminton and international championships.

'Exciting times' is how Jane Pontifex, the sport's first chief scorer and later *Horse & Hound's* first female eventing reporter, remembers Burghley in 1961. James Grose, an inspirational figure in the sport who pioneered the idea of horse and rider registrations as a means of generating revenue for the sport, was apparently a great man for graphs. And after Burghley's modest start, the graphs – for ticket sales, entries, tradestands, and so on - forever spiralled upwards.

1961

The horse that won the inaugural Burghley, the classy Merely-a-Monarch, is still held up as a blueprint for eventing breeding, and many horses from his bloodline had honourable careers in the sport in the next decades. The perfect stamp of event horse, a

bold, galloping Thoroughbred, he had already won showjumping trophies at Wembley and people told his rider, Anneli Drummond-Hay, who received numerous lucrative offers for him, that she was mad to risk him across country.

Anneli led the dressage phase at Burghley and, despite going slowly across country – she was held up on the course because it was causing so much trouble – she won by a mile, receiving her trophy from The Duke of Edinburgh. She and her brilliant mount made history as the first of an elite group of horses and riders to win Burghley and Badminton in the same 12 months, the pair going on to capture the latter event in the spring of 1962.

That was to be Anneli's last major eventing result – subsequently, she lived abroad (she is now based in Holland) and show jumped with success, winning a silver medal on Merely-a-Monarch at the world showjumping championships of 1970. Her great-niece, Izzy Taylor, is now making a name in eventing and was seventh at Burghley in 2012.

There were 19 starters for the inaugural event, but only nine completed and there were only two clear cross-country rounds, for the winner and second-placed Jeremy Smith-Bingham on By Golly. In those days, this sort of result was not uncommon; riders were allowed to continue after falls and it was worth it, because if the course caused enough trouble, they would still be placed. No one thought anything of getting back on after a mishap, and if you were riding for a team you were expected to continue even if injured, but these would not be acceptable statistics today!

Ireland's Patrick Conolly-Carew who, as Lord Carew, was to go on to judge at Burghley and to chair the FEI Eventing Committee, was third with a refusal on Ballyhoo, and dual Badminton winner and Olympic gold medallist Lt-Col Frank Weldon was fourth despite a fall on The Young Pretender.

Tradestand holders included Devon Clothing, Garrard, Herbert Johnson, Midland Bank, F. R. Gray (China), G.C. Smith Coachworks and Sturgess Land Rover, all of whom are still around today.

1962

Burghley stepped into the breach and hosted the European Championships, a competition which started at Badminton in 1953 and became bi-annual (this was the only time it ran in an even-numbered year). Four teams entered: Britain, France, Ireland and the USSR, the latter gamely driving across Europe, their horses arriving at Burghley jelly-legged. Incredibly, they won, a reflection of how prominent Russia was in eventing in the early days – now, they would be considered only minor participants in the sport and rank outsiders in a championship.

Ireland, fielding the father-daughter combination of Harry and Virginia Freeman-Jackson, took team silver and Britain the bronze, the team comprising Frank Weldon on Young Pretender, Mike Bullen, who later became famous for pioneering modern methods of flying competition horses (Sea Breeze), Susan Fleet (The Gladiator) and Peter Welch (Mister Wilson).

As host nation, Britain was allowed to field individual riders outside of the team (this is now capped at eight) and two of them won the individual gold and bronze medals. Captain James Templar of the Royal Horse Artillery and M'Lord Connolly, who went on to

win Badminton in 1964, captured the individual title. They beat the USSR's German Gazumov (Granj), and Jane Wykeham-Musgrave (Ryebrooks) took the bronze. Jane led after cross-country but suffered an expensive jumping round with five fences down.

1963

H arry Freeman-Jackson became the first and, so far, only Irish winner of Burghley, riding St Finbarr. A homeless individual, known as 'Nimpy', who lived quietly and uncommunicatively in one of the permanent stables and was something of a local institution, painted 'St. Finnibar' in his honour on the wall of the Dutch barn which housed the grooms' canteen.

Major Derek Allhusen, one of the great names of 1960s eventing, finished second of the 34 starters on Lochinvar; the pair went on to win Olympic team gold and individual silver medals at Mexico in 1968. His team mate, Sgt Ben Jones, was fifth at Burghley that year on Master Bernard, while other competitors of note included the Swede Lars Sederholm, fourth on Char's Choice – Lars went on to found a famed training centre at Waterstock in Oxfordshire, producing many of the world's greatest riders – and a young Cambridge University student called Richard Meade, who was ninth on Barberry.

1964

Richard Meade's illustrious career was put on the map with a win, his first major victory, on Barberry, a horse he described as being sensitive and cautious and therefore an educational ride that was to put him in good stead for the future. Unusually, Burghley was

timed so that places for the Olympics (in Tokyo) were still up for grabs, and this sealed Richard's place in the British team, the first of his four consecutive Olympic appearances.

Barberry, loaned to Richard by the horse's breeder, Kitty Clements, was one of the outstanding horses of the 1960s, along with Cornishman V, The Poacher and Lochinvar. He was never out of the first three and he was on the British team five times.

German rider Joachim Meherdorf was second on Iltschi, later going on to ride in the Mexico Olympics, and Ben Jones and Master Bernard were third. Another German rider, Ludwig Goessing, led the dressage, eventually finishing fifth on King – it was to be a long time before the average British rider was generally considered accomplished enough to be dangerous in the dressage phase and the Germans tended to be supreme. Joachim and Ludwig were classified as riding for West Germany although during this part of the 1960s, East and West united to form their eventing teams.

Another notable competitor was Ireland's Major Eddy Boylan, fourth on the massive Durlas Eile; they went on to be the only Irish winners of

Badminton (in 1965) and European champions in 1967. However, the times were a-changing: four of the top ten finishers were women, including the 1950s pin-up girl, Sheila Waddington (nee Willcox), 10th on Glenamoy.

1965

Despite the gradual broadening of competitor backgrounds, the military was still to the fore, and Capt Jeremy Beale, who was later based in the USA, took the honours on Victoria Bridge.

Other interesting names on the scoreboard included the runner-up, Marietta Speed (later Fox-Pitt) on Rise And Shine - her son, William, holds the record for Burghley victories (six). In fifth place was Pollyann Hely-Hutchinson (now Lochore), who went on to run the popular Scottish event at Burgie and whose son, Alec, ran the eventing competition at the London Olympic Games in 2012.

Also on the scoresheet was a young dairy farmer from Gloucestershire, Mike Tucker, who now commentates for the BBC on Burghley, among other major equestrian events.

1966

By now, Burghley was sufficiently established for the FEI (Federation Equestre Internationale), the sport's international governing body, to award it the first ever world championships in eventing. It was nearly a terrible anti-climax, though, as a swamp fever epidemic meant that no horses from Europe were allowed to come.

However, an enterprising group of Argentinian riders sailed their horses over, spending a month in quarantine on arrival in England. It seemed only fair that one of them, Capt Carlos Moratorio riding Chalan, should win the individual title. He remains Argentina's most successful ever event rider, as that country has also faded from the international equestrian picture.

The Irish won team gold – only two of the five teams completed the competition – which meant that the next world championships, in 1970, was awarded to Ireland (Punchestown). This is how designation of championships worked in those days.

Richard Meade boosted home morale with his first individual medal, silver, on Barberry, and Virginia

Right: *Rising stars – future winners Mark Phillips and Jane Bullen (aboard Our Nobby) flank Caroline Northay and Elizabeth Dotesio. The quartet were members of the Duke of Beaufort's team at the Pony Club Championships in 1965.*

Freeman-Jackson won the bronze for Ireland on the consistent team horse Sam Weller.

1967

Scottish rider Lorna Sutherland (later Clarke) sprang onto the international scene with a win on the cheeky skewbald cob Popadom, who remains the only coloured horse to win a four-star event. He was actually a grandson of the great racing sire Hyperion, but his hogged mane and chunky appearance were a long way from what is considered the classic event horse nowadays, although in those early days the sport was considered, as the Duke of Beaufort said, 'just the sort of activity for a good English hunter'.

Popadom was bought as a foal with his mother for £40; his new owner, Jennifer Harrison, had to fend off competition from Chipperfield Circus at the sale. He led the dressage phase at Burghley and, although his lack of blood began to tell on the speed and endurance phases, he perked up when he saw the deer in the park. He received many admiring visitors to the stables that night. Next day, he showjumped

clear and then bucked all the way through prize-giving.

It was Lorna's first time at Burghley, and she was eliminated in the showjumping phase on her other ride, Nicholas Nickleby, for taking the wrong course. She went on to make 17 appearances at Burghley and she became a mainstay of the British team. Lorna's other claim to fame in the 1960s was being the only woman to ride three horses around Badminton in one year – nowadays riders are restricted to only two rides at Badminton and Burghley.

Entries topped the 40-mark for the first time, with 47 runners, of which 27 completed. Lorna beat the successful show jumper Althea Roger-Smith, who would later marry the champion jockey and trainer Josh Gifford – their daughter, Kristina Cook, became European champion in 2009 and an established member of the British team but she has, so far, not bettered her mother's Burghley record.

It was an all-girl line-up, as third place was occupied by Mike Bullen's sister Jane (now Mrs Holderness-Roddam), who was then working full time as an obstetric nurse at the Middlesex Hospital. Jane's mount, the family horse

Our Nobby, who stood barely 15hh, was another untypical event horse, but in 1968 he won Badminton, was third again at Burghley, and was a member of Britain's gold-medal team at the Mexico Olympics in one of the most romantic stories in eventing history. It is extremely unusual now for a rider at the top of the tree in eventing to have a full-time job in a non-equestrian profession (Germany's Hinrich Romeike, the 2008 Olympic gold medallist, who is a dentist, is a rare exception).

Jane's future Olympic team mate, Derek Allhusen, was fifth on Lochinvar, behind another name for the future, Mark Phillips, fourth on Rock On. For the first time, Burghley hosted riders from the Far East. A trio of Japanese riders, in training for the 1968 Olympics, entered: the most successful, Mikio Chiba, finished 13th on Josephine.

1968

Sheila Willcox (back riding under her maiden name) made a dramatic comeback to the forefront of eventing, with victory on Fair and Square. Sheila, who won a record hat-trick of Badminton victories in 1957-59

Far Left: *Lorna Sutherland (now Clark) parades the cob Popadom at the Horse of the Year Show in 1967. Popadom is the only skewbald horse to have won a four-star event.*

and the European title in 1967, was considered ahead of her time in terms of professional approach to the sport: she had trained in Germany, she understood the importance of flatwork as a training aid, and she was immaculately prepared, both physically and mentally.

Sheila was arguably the first real professional event rider (although no one termed themselves professional if they wanted to ride in the Olympics), but she also had a controversial relationship with the team selectors, which included Frank Weldon, and she was embittered that women were barred from the Olympics. Her chance finally came in 1968, but she had a fall at the final team trial and was only named as reserve, a decision she could not swallow, so she declined to travel to Mexico. Later, a bad fall thwarted any serious continuation in the sport and she turned to dealing and training, but she remains one of the legends of eventing.

Two horses that did go to Mexico featured in that 1968 line-up: Cornishman V, one of the greatest ever event horses, was eighth with Sgt Ben Jones – his rider, Mary Gordon Watson, had broken her leg – and The Poacher,

the only horse to win both Great and Little Badminton, was 11th with his owner, Martin Whiteley.

Mr Whiteley, an Eton beak, had won European team gold and individual silver medals on The Poacher in 1967, but back trouble put paid to his eventing career and he generously loaned the horse, first to Sgt Ben Jones, who won an Olympic team gold medal on him in Mexico, and to Richard Meade, who won Badminton on the horse in 1970. Mr Whiteley was chairman of the Combined Training Committee, the selection committee, and the Horse Trials Support Group, which he helped found. Tragically, he died far too young, while out on a run at Eton in 1984.

1969

This year marked the greatest riding triumph for Gill Watson, who quickly became renowned as a trainer of under-21 riders. Under her auspices, Britain's Young Rider team, which she trained until 2011, dominated their European championships with an incredible medal haul – her charges included Karen Straker (later Dixon), William Fox-Pitt, Pippa Funnell and

Kristina Gifford.

Gill was not from a horsey background – she learned to ride at boarding school – and formed a special partnership with her winning horse, Shaitan. An Arab-hunter cross, she broke him in herself for her Pony Club district commissioner and finished sixth at her first attempt at Burghley in 1968, after which the pair were travelling reserves (instead of Sheila Willcox) for the British Olympic team in Mexico.

At the start of 1969, the pair had an unsuccessful outing to Punchestown and Gill, who had only recently left school to train as a PE teacher, had no expectations of doing well at Burghley. Lorna Sutherland lay first and second after dressage on Popadom and Gypsy Flame; Gill was third at that stage on Shaitan but she, and eventual runner-up Mike Tucker on Skyborn, were significantly faster across country. Gill's advantage over Mike, who was only 17th after dressage, was enough for her to have four show jumps down (as against his two) and still win.

Scoreboards in the 1960s show the extraordinary influence the cross-country had in those days, despite its relative lack of combination fences.

However, the sport was to enter a new and competive era in the golden 1970s.

RIDER OF THE DECADE

Richard Meade

Richard Meade, who became a mainstay of the British eventing team for 20 years, was an eight-year-old boy when the first Badminton took place in 1949, but he was completely entranced by proceedings and knew, from that moment, that he wanted to compete at the highest level himself. Born near Chepstow, in Wales, he came from an equestrian, rural family – his parents were joint-masters of the Curre foxhounds – and competed as a child. He took an engineering degree at Cambridge, was briefly in the army and worked in the City, all the while riding a great variety of horses, some talented, some not, for different owners.

In those days, the best riders were matched to the best horses available for the good of the country, regardless of who owned them, and Richard became known as an adaptable, intelligent and competitive horseman, with a strong sense of commitment to the British

team. His Burghley victory on his own Barberry in 1964 (oddly, he never won the event again) was to be the start of great things: the pair were chosen for the Tokyo Olympics that year and, although the team was eliminated, Richard finished the best, in eighth place.

In 1968, he rode Mary Gordon Watson's Cornishman V, a horse he had never sat on before, to finish fourth individually and win team gold at the Mexico Olympics, and in 1972 he won team and individual gold at the Munich Olympics on Derek Allhusen's Laurieston, who was known to be a tricky horse. He was the highest-placed member of the British team at the Munich Olympics in 1976 and the disastrous World Championships at Kentucky in 1978.

Richard also won three European team gold medals and two World team gold medals, plus Badminton twice, in 1970 on The Poacher and in 1972 on Speculator. He went on to become a top-level judge and trainer, an FEI official and a field master for the Duke of Beaufort's hounds. He now works as an expert witness in equestrian-related court cases and helps his son, Harry, who now competes.

Right: A hatless
Virginia Freeman-
Jackson flies
across country on
Sam Weller. They
were members of
the winning Irish
team at the World
Championships in
1966.

The 1970s

The 1970s are still considered the Golden Age of eventing. British riders dominated the sport in Europe with gold medals galore, and glamorous figures such as Richard Meade and Lucinda Prior-Palmer (now Green) became household names. There was royal participation, through Princess Anne and her dashing soldier husband, Capt Mark Phillips, the Queen came to watch them, and the media loved it. *Horse & Hound*, the bible for the sport, was at its height, with circulation figures hitting the 90,000s; all the major newspapers had dedicated equestrian correspondents and ran sports reports of national one-day events, and event riders, including the Princess, were regulars on *A Question of Sport*.

Sponsorship began to take off, and the sport attracted significant investment from the Midland Bank, an enthusiastic, discreet and generous backer of many events and national championships in the British calendar until the mid-1980s. The first financial backing at Burghley was provided by Bass and then Raleigh.

With heightened awareness there came also, perhaps, the first real criticism of a British team, when commentators suggested that complacency had set in after the Americans, who appeared to be taking a more streamlined and strategic approach, won the 1974 World Championships and 1976 Olympics. The wholesale disaster of the 1978 World Championships in Kentucky was

also to engender a change in attitude for the whole sport.

The administration of the national sport in Britain expanded, too, with a burgeoning national calendar of some 150 events. Balloting had to be introduced for the most popular events and late withdrawals were frowned upon; riders had to produce a veterinary certificate on their second 'offence' which could carry an automatic suspension for three months.

Computerised scoring arrived in its earliest form, under the efficient auspices of the late and much missed Jacqui Mason, aided by Paul Harris. A more refined version of that original system is still the blueprint today. However, organisers resisted the idea of a central entry system based in head office as they wished to retain control of their own entries. Horse registration fees were £2 and entry fees £4.

1970

Judy Bradwell, one of a generation of smartly-turned out female graduates of the show pony ring, won Burghley on Don Camillo, a horse previously

Above: *Mary Gordon Watson and Mark Phillips walk the Trout Hatchery fence at the 1971 European Championships*

ridden by Debbie West. Judy led from the start with a brilliant dressage test. She was one of the most prolific winners on the national circuit then and went on to become a top-level judge, including at Burghley (she was the first British woman to judge at a world championships, in 1994), and a fine producer of both young horses and young riders.

Another former showing rider and now eminent lady judge was also in the prizes, Angela Sowden (who soon afterwards married fellow rider Mike Tucker) in sixth place on Mooncoin. Other prize-winners of note included the runner-up, South African-born Richard Walker on Upper Strata – the previous year he set the record as the youngest ever winner of Badminton, aged 18 – and, in fifth, the enduring partnership of Debbie West and Baccarat.

1971

Burghley hosted the European Championships, which resulted in a British clean sweep of the medals and an historic royal victory for Princess Anne riding Doublet. She led the field of 45 from the start, finishing with a clear show jumping round to clinch the trophy which was presented, amid fairytale scenes of jubilation, by her mother, The Queen. As far as publicity went, it couldn't get much better than that for the sport.

Trained by Alison Oliver, Princess Anne began competing in senior horse trials in 1968 on Purple Star, a horse bred by the Crown Equerry, Sir John Miller, and whose dam, Stella, was ridden by Bertie Hill in the 1952 Olympics. Doublet, a bright chestnut gelding bred by The Queen, later tragically broke a leg while schooling on the flat in Windsor Great Park and was put down.

It was a British whitewash. The team (Debbie West and Baccarat, the individual silver medallists, Mary Gordon Watson on Cornishman V, Richard Meade on The Poacher and Mark Phillips on Great Ovation) took gold, beating the USSR and Ireland by more than 400 points, and British riders won all three individual medals.

In those days, riders rarely achieved the optimum cross-country time at Burghley, but the Bertie Hill-trained Stuart Stevens, a young Exmoor farmer who had experience of point-to-pointing, rose from 35th place after dressage to take bronze on Classic Chips with the only cross-country round in single-figure time penalties.

Seven teams contested the championships, including a Dutch team of which Eddy Stibbe was a member (he retired on Phase D on Autumn Bronze). Eddy was to become a fixture in Britain, a generous benefactor to the sport and a host to several nations for training at his Waresley Park Stud in Bedfordshire. At one stage, he had competed at more events than any other rider, and he continued eventing until he was 60.

Burghley 1971 was notable for the arrival of a new scoring system, which is still used in the sport today. Previously, a rider's final score was worked out by subtracting the dressage score from the overall jumping penalties – the person with the highest score of plus points won. From 1971, all penalties have been added to make a total, with the lowest total winning.

1972

Olympic contenders swelled the field and the number of starters rose dramatically to 71 (42 completed), the highest since 1967, although it slumped down again until 1979. Burghley has so often provided a chance to shine for riders who didn't make the cut for the team championships, and in 1972, the year of the Munich Olympics, it was the career highlight for one of the leading combinations of the day, Janet Hodgson and Larkspur. They were only 11th after dressage, but very fast over an influential cross-country course.

Janet's most famous moment, however, was at the following year's European Championships in Kiev when she suffered two cross-country falls but continued to the end of the course, despite suffering facial injuries, for which the Russians gave her a bravery award.

Debbie West, whose Baccarat suffered an untimely lameness at the last minute at the Munich Olympics, was second at Burghley, and there were two other notable faces in the final line-up: an 18-year-old Lucinda Prior-Palmer was fourth on her Pony Club and Junior horse, Be Fair, and Germany's Olympic medallist Horst Karsten and the great Sioux were sixth.

Bill Roycroft, hero of the Australian Olympic team in 1960, became the first from his country to ride at Burghley, but he withdrew his horse, Harley, on the third day.

1973

Geldings have always dominated the highest levels of eventing – most riders prefer them, finding them simpler to manage - and only two mares have won Burghley, 33 years apart. In 1973, Bertie Hill's mare Maid Marion was the first. She should have been ridden by Bertie's son, Tony, but he had injured his back in a fall and so the catch ride went to Mark Phillips in the year he married Princess Anne. Alongside Richard Meade, Capt Phillips was the great horseman of his day and the two were often closely matched; Capt Phillips won Badminton four times but, surprisingly, Burghley only once, although he has become intrinsically linked to the event in his role as course-designer.

Diana Thorne, one of the pioneering amateur lady jockeys of the day (she later married the successful racehorse trainer,

Above: Capt Mark Phillips riding Maid Marion, winner in 1973

Nicky Henderson), was second on the grey The Kingmaker; Sue Hatherley (as Sue Benson, she went on to become a leading female course-designer who produced the track at the London Olympic Games) was third on Harley and businessman Chris Collins, who perhaps epitomised more than anyone the Corinthian spirit of the age, was fourth on Centurian.

Chris was a key member of the British team in the 1970s and, alongside his demanding career as head of Goya, he made history as the first Briton to win the fearsome Pardubice Steeplechase in Czechoslovakia and was also third in the Grand National on Stephen's Society.

Another rider who was to make her name in National Hunt racing was Henrietta Knight, who rode Blitzkrieg into 24th place. 'Hen' was later chairman of selectors and famously trained Best Mate to win three Cheltenham Gold Cups.

1974

Burghley hosted the World Championships, in honour of the British team having won double gold at the 1970 running in Punchestown, Ireland. They were favourites to win again, but a combination of bad luck and the sudden emergence of the USA as a force in the sport relegated them to silver, ahead of Germany in bronze. The German team included Martin Plewa, seventh on Virginia – Martin is now well known as a judge and technical delegate in the sport and has officiated many times at Burghley.

British hopes were high when Mark Phillips and the team were in the lead after cross-country, but disaster struck when Mark's horse, the powerful grey Columbus Vl, owned by his mother-in-law The Queen, slipped a tendon off his hock and had to be withdrawn overnight. It was probably the greatest disappointment of Mark's riding career, as he describes Columbus as the best horse he ever rode.

Instead, it was the rising star Bruce Davidson who took individual gold medal on Irish Cap, led his team to victory and rode off on the Raleigh bicycle given by the sponsor. Bruce, a member of the silver medal team at the Munich Olympics, came over to compete at Badminton in 1974 as part of his honeymoon and finished third on Irish Cap.

A striking-looking man with blond hair and azure eyes, Bruce, who gave up veterinary training to compete full time, soon became known as a talented and colourful personality on the eventing scene and one who was hugely organised – all the other riders would rely on him to work out the cross-country timings. Bruce is the only rider to have successfully defended his world title, which he did in 1978. He also won Olympic team gold medals in 1976 and 1984.

Bruce's team mate on those two occasions, Mike Plumb, took the individual silver medal at Burghley, on Good Mixture. The bronze went to

Above: *Bruce Davidson tries out his prize, a Raleigh bicycle*

Britain's Hugh Thomas on Playamar. Hugh is now better known as the director and course-designer at Badminton since 1989, but he was one of the leading riders in the 1970s, finishing second at Badminton and riding as a member of the Olympic team in 1976.

Bridget Parker, one of the 1972 Olympic gold medallists, was the next best placed team member, in ninth on Cornish Gold, and British riders

dominated the individual placings with Janet Hodgson fourth, Richard Meade seventh, Lucinda Prior-Palmer 10th and Toby Sturgis 11th. Princess Anne was 12th on Doublet's successor, Goodwill.

1975

Aly Pattinson, yet another graduate from show pony classes, scored the biggest win of her career with victory on Carawich, a talented and clever horse who always had 'a fifth leg'. The horse had been competed by his owner, Alex Colquhoun, who gave up eventing due to the commitments of his job in the bloodstock insurance world (he is now chairman of the British Young Rider selectors) and, to the dismay of selectors, was a few years later sold to well-known American rider Jimmy Wofford.

Nowadays, a more accepting attitude towards selling horses prevails in Britain – riders have to make a living, after all, and often a lucrative sale can be life-changing and enable them to buy property – but in those days it was expected that one's country and the team would come first.

Aly Pattinson (now Boswell) went on to organise horse trials for many years at Auchinleck in Scotland, and some

of the placed riders that year have also gone on to play significant roles in the administration of the sport. Jane Starkey, seventh on Topper Too, became a judge and event organiser; Pattie Biden, seventh on Little Extra, runs 'little' Gatcombe horse trials and is a British Eventing regional director; and Julian Seaman, 12th on Master Question, is press officer at Badminton.

1976

Jane Holderness-Roddam, who found fame as 'the galloping nurse' in the aftermath of the 1968 Mexico Olympics when she became the first British woman to win an Olympic gold medal for equestrian sport, was always the most graceful of riders. She formed a great partnership with Susie Howard's Warrior, an impressive stamp of event horse, and won both Burghley this year and Badminton in 1978 with him.

Jane described Warrior as the most intelligent horse she had ever ridden. He came from John Shedden, one of the most professional riders of his day and immortalised as the first winner of Badminton, in 1949. Jane and Warrior almost didn't make it to Burghley,

Far Right:
*Lucinda Prior-
Palmer and
George jump the
last fence on their
way to winning
the European
Chamionships in
1977*

however, as they had a frightening fall a few months earlier when the horse cartwheeled over a fence at Bramham and landed with his front hooves either side of Jane's face, pinning her hairnet to the ground. She recalls Lady Hugh Russell, who trained the British team, yelling at her not to carry on but, determined to qualify for Burghley, she leapt back on.

The drama continued at Burghley, when the pair crashed over a practice fence before the final showjumping round, in which she was lying second behind Toby Sturgis on Demi Douzaine, who knocked out a few rails. Jane had to ride into the showjumping arena with a broken breastplate which was flapping around and threatening to trip up the horse, but he still jumped a beautiful clear round.

A member of the talented and influential Bullen family, Jane is now chairman of Riding for the Disabled, president of the British Equestrian Federation and, with her sister, Jennie Loriston-Clark, the chairman of British Dressage, a leading figure in the world of sports horse breeding through her stud at West Kington, Wiltshire.

Lucinda Prior-Palmer, who had already conquered Badminton twice and won a European title, had yet to triumph at Burghley, but this year she came very close, in second place on the chunky Killaire, a horse not ideally built for eventing but whose 'middle name was try'.

It was an end of an era when James Grose, the man who put Burghley on the map, stepped down as director. Major Andrew Burnaby-Atkins took over, although, sadly, ill health meant he only stayed for two years.

1977

Lucinda Prior-Palmer was to set many records in eventing, some of which remain unbroken, and here she made history as the first rider to defend her European title successfully. It was a courageous performance as she was suffering from both flu and depression after the death of her beloved father Major-General Errol Prior-Palmer, who was a wise and senior figure in the sport.

Her mount, Elaine Straker's George, was not the easiest of rides – he was clever, but not particularly careful and had had a few falls with Elaine's sons – and he felt similarly lethargic on cross country day. Lucinda felt so weak and lacking in confidence that she fell off on the steeplechase and was dragged along, but fortunately this occurred outside the penalty zone around the fence, so did not incur penalties, and, after remounting, she was still inside the time allowed.

Again, on the cross-country phase, Lucinda felt like giving up, but one of the spectators, a gentleman standing beside the ropes, raised his shooting stick in the air and shouted: 'Come on England, come on George!' This served as the necessary shot in the arm, and she galloped home to spearhead another British team gold. Lucinda's team mates Jane Holderness-Roddam, on Warrior, and Chris Collins on Smokey were fifth and seventh respectively; Clarissa Strachan's Merry Sovereign had to be withdrawn.

Karl Schultz riding Madrigal led for Germany after dressage and cross-country, but two show jumps down relegated him to the silver medal. His compatriot Horst Karsten on Sioux took bronze and the Germans collected the team silver medal.

Seven nations fielded teams. Ireland won bronze, and the quartet included the Eton-educated John Watson, who

worked as a land agent at Burghley, on the great Cambridge Blue, winners of the individual silver medal at the next year's World Championships behind Bruce Davidson. Just as Bruce's son Buck is now regularly competing at four-star level, so John's son Sam made his Burghley debut in 2012.

1978

Charles Stratton, who had been involved with Burghley since its inception, took over as director, and continued to increase Burghley's status as a major sporting spectacular. The event hosted its first under-21 championship, the Junior Europeans, but the host nation didn't get a look in. West Germany won team gold, with their Dietrich Baumgart and Ralf Ehrenbrink scooping individual gold and silver medals – the latter was later famously a member of the all-conquering German team at the 1988 Seoul Olympics.

The best-placed British rider was Christopher Bealby, member of a well-known Leicestershire hunting family, in eighth place on Jack Be Nimble; his father, Jim, was a committee member at Burghley for many years.

Left: Jane Holderness-Roddam and Warrior, the 1978 winners, pictured during the 1977 European championships when they were members of the gold medal team

The newly married Lorna Clarke (nee Sutherland) was the popular winner of the 'real thing', riding her own Greco. It was a particularly good story because Lorna had been through a fallow patch and worried that she might have lost her nerve; Greco, a horse she described as 'a perfect gent' was nearly sold to Canada but had failed the vet. Second place went to one of the great dressage exponents of the day, Rachel Bayliss, on Gurgle the Greek.

Lorna, the first rider to win Burghley twice, was one of the most versatile riders of her era, and at one stage held the record for the most completions of Burghley (15 between 1967 and 1987) until overtaken by New Zealander Andrew Nicholson.

The year 1978 was a memorable one for horse trials for all the wrong reasons: the World Championships in Kentucky were catastrophic, due to the high humidity, and produced distressing pictures of horses finishing the cross-country in a state of collapse. It was agreed that nothing like this must ever happen again in the sport, and the result was a far more stringent inspection of championship venues – countries now have to bid for these and demonstrate proper forethought – and beneficial developments in veterinary care.

Transporting a team to the USA from Britain was also prohibitively expensive and this spawned the arrival of the Horse Trials Support Group, which was founded by Martin Whiteley with Tom Greenhalgh, Chris Collins, Tim Holderness-Roddam and Jane Pontifex, and aimed to raise funds to send British eventing teams to overseas championships.

1979

Australian and New Zealand riders are now an integral part of the British eventing scene, but back in the 1970s they had yet to make their presence felt, apart from the raiding party of Aussies who sailed over in 1960 and wiped the Brits' eyes at Badminton and the Olympics that year.

Therefore, Andrew Hoy, a 20-year-old dairy farmer from New South Wales and the sole Australian in the field, was something of a shock winner on his little stock horse, Davey, especially as, with field of 75, it was the most competitive entry for seven years. Based with Princess Anne and Mark Phillips at Gatcombe

Andrew had ridden at the World Championships the year before and, like many enterprising antipodeans after him, decided that as Britain was the epicentre of the sport and the place to be, although it was to be many years before he finally settled in England.

New Zealander Mark Todd, another dairy farmer, had followed the same path and made his Burghley debut in the same year, completing in 35th place with two refusals on Jocasta. Both men were to become dominant in the sport and inspire generations of their countrymen, but then, amid all the very English accents, their lack of tweed and antipodean twangs were something of a novelty.

Only two riders achieved the optimum cross-country time that year – Andrew Hoy and another overseas visitor, who has also become a fixture in

LITTLE BOOK OF **BURGHLEY**

British eventing. Goran 'Yogi' Briesner, who was based at fellow Swede Lars Sederholm's influential training centre at Waterstock, finished fifth on his best horse Ultimus. Two decades later, he was, to great acclaim, to become the manager – and face – of Britain's eventing teams.

RIDER OF THE DECADE

Lucinda Green

Ask any rider over age of 30 who their inspiration is, and they will invariably name Lucinda Green (nee Prior-Palmer). Dazzlingly attractive and with an ebullient and kind personality and athletic physique, her riding style was distinctive and charismatic. Her seat on a horse was notable for its determinedly strong lower leg and she had an elastic style of slipping the reins and giving the horse the freedom of its head. Above all, she made it look fun.

In her day, the idea of the typical four-star event horse – with the stamina and speed of the Thoroughbred and the movement and jumping style of the warmblood – had not taken hold, and the Burghley horse came in all shapes and sizes, as evinced by Jane Bullen's pony, Nobby, or Lorna Sutherland's skewbald cob, Popadom. Lucinda will, therefore, always be most famous for being successful on so many different horses, of all shapes and sizes and wildly differing levels of talent. Her record of winning Badminton six times on six different horses, between 1973 and 1984, is unlikely to be surpassed.

She represented Britain at seven European championships. The horse that brought her to prominence was a smart little chestnut called Be Fair, who she produced from Pony Club level; they won Badminton in 1973 and the European Championships in 1975. His career ended tragically when he slipped a tendon off his hock at the 1976 Olympics in Montreal.

Perhaps her best horse was the last of the big winners, the Australian stock horse Regal Realm, winner of the World Championships in 1982 and Badminton in 1984, plus a team silver medal at the Los Angeles Olympics. Here, an average dressage mark precluded higher honours – it is fair to say that it was the cross-country phase for which she became so famous and, rightly, earned many plaudits.

Far Left: A youthful Andrew Hoy wins Burghley at his first attempt in 1979 on Davey, an Australian stock horse.

Above: *A 25-year-old Lucinda Prior-Palmer receives her MBE at Buckingham Palace in 1978.*

Lucinda married the Australian rider David Green in 1981 (they divorced a decade later) and has two children, Freddie and Lissa, who now has her own eventing yard. Lucinda is in great demand worldwide as a trainer and commentator and she still competes in horse trials – the sight of her primrose-yellow colours approaching across country is still a thrill for spectators.

Left: *"Come on England, come on George!" A galvanized Lucinda Prior-Palmer (now Green) and George on their lap of honour in 1977.*

The 1980s

The booming prosperity, innovation and ambition of the Thatcher years was reflected in horse trials, as businessmen decided that eventing could be a glamorous and entertaining day out. Corporate sponsorship poured in at all levels of the sport, some of it brought in by Princess Anne and Capt Mark Phillips at Gatcombe.

British riders were continuing to give tremendous value for money: the senior team was at its zenith, winning the world championships in 1982 and 1986 plus four European championships, team silvers at both the 1984 and 1988 Olympic Games and a plethora of individual medals, especially for Ginny Holgate, Ian Stark and Lorna Clarke.

As a result, the sport was still receiving plenty of attention from the media; the BBC televised an imaginative challenge, devised by Mark Phillips, in which National Hunt jockeys including Richard Dunwoody, Steve Smith-Eccles and Simon Sherwood rode across country at Gatcombe and eventers such as Rodney Powell and Mark Todd took on the Grand National fences at Aintree.

In 1981, the under-21 end of the sport, promoted as a training ground for future senior team riders, underwent a restructuring with the creation, prompted and devised by Britain' Christopher Schofield, of a Young Rider European Championship for

riders aged 19–21. Trained by the 1969 Burghley winner, Gill Watson, Britain's teams swept the board in this category, too.

There were changes to the old order at the highest level when Bill Thomson, very much a father-figure to up-and-coming course-designers, stepped down at Burghley in 1984 – he was succeeded by Philip Herbert, who is still clerk of the course at Burghley – and the inimitable Frank Weldon retired from

efficient director, Bill elevated the event to even higher levels, engendering a sharp, if good-humoured, rivalry with Badminton. He liked to bill himself as 'a simple Lincolnshire farmer', but the truth was that he was a shrewd businessman and creative showman who understood that spectators were not mere adjuncts to the main action but central to its healthy finances and vibrant atmosphere.

An approachable and friendly man, Bill recognised that organised car-parking, ample loos and varied, well-placed catering were crucial to enjoyment of a day out, and he inspected prospective tradestands rigorously for quality and presentation. He regularly visited overseas events, admiring the ones that were professionally fronted, stylish and had healthy sponsorship, especially in France, and, on his return, was assiduous in his efforts to replicate the tactical branding and value for money to sponsors.

Although Bill always listened to what riders had to say, he generally expected other officials to get the sporting side right and to take care of the rules and fair judgements. Unlike some other organisers, he did not get involved in course-design, instead promoting the

Badminton in 1988, to be succeeded by Hugh Thomas. Frank died soon after, in 1989, and Bill in 1993.

In 1987, Bill Henson took over from Charles Stratton as director of Burghley. If Charles had been a progressive and idea that this was an international skill and that it did no harm to swap people around, introduce new styles and test new formats.

1980

Richard Walker, who grew up riding Basuto ponies in South Africa, had spent 11 years riding under the tag 'youngest winner of Badminton' (at 18), so it must have come as a relief when he won Burghley in 1980 on Kent Leather Distribution's John of Gaunt.

Richard, one of the most high-profile, precise and accomplished products of Lars Sederholm's Waterstock centre, was probably at the height of his career at the time. John of Gaunt was a genuine and enthusiastic horse but, due to his breeding – he was by a Cleveland Bay stallion belonging to The Queen – wasn't built for terrific speed. His owner, Ken Lyndon Dykes, rode him until the horse's fear of tractors caused him a broken arm.

Mark Phillips led the dressage and cross-country phases on Range Rover Team's Persian Holidays (note the proliferation of corporate ownership of horses) but hit two show jumps in the final phase to slip to second.

Jane Holderness-Roddam was third on the wonderful Warrior, and the event was notable for the emergence of Ginny Holgate in sixth place. Ginny was second after dressage but incurred 27.2 time penalties across country on Priceless. It was probably the last time they did so – Ginny's peers would describe their fluent, corner-cutting across country, in perfect synchronicity, as looking like a motorbike and its rider.

The field this year was the most competitive yet – 79 starters – a record which was to last for another 20 years. Nowadays, 80-plus starters are the norm.

1981

In the spirit of the age, the winning and second-placed horses were again corporately owned. Lucinda Prior-Palmer, who by this stage was engaged to the young Australian David Green, won on Beagle Bay, owned by Overseas Containers Ltd. Beagle Bay, who provided Lucinda with her sixth Badminton win, in 1984, was a cocky, sweet-looking grey horse who could be naughty at a practice fence but was

Right: Ginny Holgate, whose brilliant career was just taking off, and dynamic Burghley director Charles Stratton

brave in the real thing.

Richard Meade was second on Speculator lll, owned by George Wimpey, on which he went on to win Badminton the following year. Ginny Holgate, still waiting in the wings, continued to progress with third place on Night Cap ll and earned her first place on a British team with Priceless.

To mark the event's 21st running, Lucinda presented Lord Exeter with a painting as recognition for all he had done to support what was rapidly becoming a world-renowned three-day event. Sadly, it was also to be his last appearance as president, as both he and Lady Exeter died within the next 12 months.

1982

Richard Walker was back on the winner's rostrum, this time aboard

Ryan's Cross. The horse was owned by Mrs Ambler, sister of the King of Sweden. Richard described his cross-country ride on the day as being like driving a Rolls Royce, but the horse was notoriously chicken about jumping ditches and Richard had prepared him by finding a different-looking ditch to jump each day.

Lizzie Purbrick, one of the great personalities at Burghley who then lived and hunted in the area, was second on Big Fry.

1983

Remy Martin arrived as title sponsor of Burghley, bringing with them new levels of glamour and sophistication with their smart branding and welcome product distribution, especially to the press. Their arrival also challenged the course-designing team as the idea of themed cross-country fences in imaginative shapes began to take hold.

Bill Thomson designed a huge timber 'brandy glass' where Ginny Holgate took a breathtakingly perfect line on Priceless, jumping the two curving rails of the 'bowl' of the glass and the corner where the 'stem' met the 'foot' of the glass without a single break in their rhythm.

The pair went on to deliver the big win everyone had been waiting for. They finished on their dressage score of 25.6 penalties, an outstanding result, and beat senior rider Richard Meade on Kilcashel by 6.2 penalties. Priceless was to become one of the all time great event horses; he never incurred a single cross-country fault and he won nine medals, six of them gold.

Both he and Night Cap ll were bred by Diana Scott, a farmer's wife and master of the Devon & Somerset Staghounds, from the Brendon hills in West Somerset who had herself competed. Priceless and Night Cap were by her stallion Ben Faerie, who sired several other successful event horses, helping to further greater interest in eventing bloodlines and breeding specifically for the sport.

Burghley also hosted the Young Rider European Championships this year, in which the dominant British team won gold, beating France and Ireland. Karen Straker (now Dixon), whose family owned the 1977 Burghley winner, George, kicked off her illustrious British team career with an individual silver medal on Running Bear and Polly Schwerdt took silver on Dylan. The individual title went, by just one point, to France's John-Paul St Vignes riding Jocelyn A.

A notable addition to Burghley's structure was the arrival of Lady Victoria Leatham, daughter of Lord Exeter, as horse trials president. An expert in fine art, with an engaging television persona, Lady Victoria was a hugely popular host, always smiling and encouraging and appearing to thoroughly enjoy the massive annual invasion into her parkland.

1984

Ginny's star was in the ascendant again, this time on Night Cap ll, a far more insecure character in comparison to Priceless who had a tendency to 'blow up' in the dressage phase.

Women filled eight out of the top 10 places and only Richard Meade, seventh on Milton General, and an up-and-coming Rodney Powell, 10th on Pomeroy, got a look in.

One of the most charming Burghley stories occurred this year when Sam Barr, best known as a mover and shaker in the world of sports horse breeding, fulfilled a lifetime's ambition by becoming the oldest rider (at 64) to compete at Burghley. Riding Welton Friday, all was going well until he lost his way in the showjumping phase and was eliminated. However, his achievement was so popular that the event still awarded him his completion plaque.

It was also the end of an era when Bill Thomson, one of the wisest advisors ever to touch the sport, retired. He handed over to Philip Herbert, although he remained as course consultant, and his influence still permeates cross-country course design today as his successors remember that their primary role is to educate horses and riders and to provide them with an enjoyable, confidence-building experience.

1985

Britain swept the board in the European Championships held at Burghley, in which nine teams competed, winning team gold and all three individual medals. Ginny won the first of many individual gold medals, on

Priceless, Lorna Clark won silver on Myross and Ian Stark, arguably the best rider never to have won Burghley, took bronze on Oxford Blue, the nearest he ever got to a win here.

France took silver, the team including France's most successful ever female rider, the stylish Marie-Christine Duroy, seventh, and Jean Teulere,

eighth. The latter, who went on to win the 2002 World title and is still competing in his 60s, received a rousing cheer as the first rider to clear the direct route at Philip Herbert's fearsome fourth fence, a bullfinch beyond a ditch.

For the first time, Ginny took on the pressurised anchorman position in the team as last to go. As with the pathfinder

spot, this has to be filled by a reliable combination. The rider needs to be able to keep a cool head, particularly if another member of the team has already fallen by the wayside as the fourth rider needs to complete to keep the team in the competition.

Priceless, a bossy, characterful horse, was not above bucking at inopportune moments, and he nearly dislodged Ginny in front of an enormous trakehner fence. There was also a difficult angled combination three from home where Ginny had been instructed by team chef d'equipe Malcolm Wallace to take the long route if she was up on the clock. She was, indeed, up on time but, confessing to never looking at her stopwatch, she decided she'd better take the straight route. This was, of course, completed with aplomb, but watching team officials had their hearts in their mouths.

1986

Ginny 's fourth consecutive Burghley victory was also the most dramatic. She was riding Murphy Himself, a grey tearaway who was only eight years old at the time – now

Right: *Ginny Holgate desperately tries to rein in the exuberant Murphy Himself*

eight-year-olds are rarely seen at four-star events, due to the difficulty of qualifying them by that stage, and many would consider it too soon anyway, but in the early days of the sport it was quite normal. They led throughout, beating the brilliant combination of Bruce Davidson and JJ Babu by just 0.8 of a penalty.

Murphy's cross-country round became progressively more alarming, as Ginny desperately grappled with the brakes, taking a shorter and shorter rein. It was all to no avail, as Murphy became flatter and more on the forehand, taking strides out wherever he felt like it with Ginny somehow courageously managing to stay with him. It is something of an irony that with a similar display in today's more politically sensitive and safety-conscious world she could have ended up as a topic of conversation on dangerous riding and been reprimanded by stewards.

Ian Stark was fourth that year on Glenburnie, another grey tearaway, and two years later, he and Ginny famously swapped horses. Ginny had broken her ankle in a fall at Badminton, when Murphy leapt from the top of the Ski Jump, and her family decided enough

was enough. Ginny took on Griffin, a somewhat less exciting chestnut horse, and Ian built a flamboyant partnership with Murphy, winning double silver medals at the 1990 World Equestrian Games and finishing second at Badminton in 1991.

1987

Mark Todd won both Badminton (in 1980) and an Olympic gold medal (in 1984) at his first attempt, but Burghley took him a little longer. However, when he did achieve victory there, he made history as the first rider to finish first and second there.

He won on Wilton Fair, a big, strong chestnut horse who was later sold to America's David O'Connor, and finished second on Charisma, the extraordinary talented little horse with whom he will forever be linked. The result would have the other way round had not Charisma, something of a careless show-off in the jumping arena, hit two fences.

To this day, Mark regrets this result; despite Charisma winning two Olympic gold medals and numerous other competitions, he was destined

to always finish in the runner–up spot in the British four-star events. As if to show his annoyance, Charisma – known also as Podge for his healthy appetite - has his ears back in all the presentation pictures.

It was another female–dominated line-up, apart from Rodney Powell in fifth on the Irishman. Diana (Tiny) Clapham was third on Jimney Cricket, Mark's fellow Kiwi, the graceful horsewoman Tinks Pottinger, was fourth on Volunter and sixth on Graphic, and Mary Thomson (now King) was at the start of her illustrious career in ninth on King Boris.

Notably, eight out of the top 10 horses were owned by corporate sponsors, such as Merrill Lynch, Carphone Group and Happy Eater.

It was Bill Henson's first year as director and an early innovation was

routing the cross-country course through the main arena for the first time, the idea being that spectators could rest their legs for a bit while still watching the action, a concept since adopted by several other events. There were also smart new hospitality suites overlooking the arena. Philip Herbert designed a testing combination fence for them to watch in the shape of the sponsor's initials, R.M., which was then removed in time for the following day's show jumping.

Another invention was the Burghley Young Event Horse series, which had qualifiers at several events and shows during the season and a finale at Burghley. The class became a showpiece for four- and five-year-old potential event horses, which were judged on comformation, movement and flatwork, and jumping. Some of Britain's greatest

Above: *Lady Hugh Russell, who was such a major influence on the British team at that time, in her "mini-moke"*

Right: *Ian
Stark (GBR)
and Glenburnie
boldly take on the
direct route at the
S-fence, allegedly
for a bet*

event horses, like General Jock, ridden by Kristina Gifford, and Primmore's Pride, ridden by Pippa Funnell, were first in the spotlight in the finale. It was sponsored for many years by Pet Plan Insurance and is now backed by Dubarry.

1988

Jane Thelwall was one of the most able horsewomen around in the 1980s, her all-round skills honed in the show ring and riding out racehorses. She was deeply disappointed not to be selected for the Olympics that year, but had her moment in the sun when she won Burghley on Kings Jester and collected the first prize of £6,000.

Jane, who was plagued by back trouble, gave up eventing soon after and went on to marry Major Malcolm Wallace, director of the British Equestrian Federation and later chairman of Burghley. She wrote equestrian books, judged and trained several riders. Kings Jester, owned by John and Maryan Huntridge, was a delightful horse who, despite shoeing problems, was successful when ridden for the Dutch team by Mandy Stibbe and then for Britain by Lorna Clarke.

Second place went to Madeleine Gurdon on Midnight Monarch. An accomplished rider of that era, she subsequently married the composer Andrew Lloyd Webber and is now chairman of the Pony Club.

Bill Henson's innovations that year included placing a big screen in the arena, which showed all the action; this was preceded by assiduous rehearsal on the Wednesday to ensure that it would not be too distracting for horses. The horse inspections were moved to the main arena, and a new computer programme showed the scoring on the screen. There were also fence analysis sheets and final scores could now be printed off within the hour.

Sadly, however, cross-country day at Burghley 1988 will always be remembered for the death of Mark Davies. A tense silence descended on proceedings after he and his horse, Normas, fell at the coffin fence, and eventually news filtered through that they had both been killed. At that stage, the shadow of fatalities had not yet fallen over the sport; indeed, it was almost unknown. Mark was a member of a shrinking breed: those who had full-time jobs outside the horse world (he worked in the City) and evented for fun and for thrills. He was described in *Eventing magazine* as 'a brave young man who in an earlier generation one could imagine at the controls of a Spitfire'.

Mark's mother, Jane Davies, threw herself into promoting higher standards of safety in riding and eventing and into helping the families of injured riders. Thus the Mark Davies Injured Riders Fund, a still successful charity, was born.

1989

Another European Championships, another two gold medals for Ginny Holgate (now Leng) and another British whitewash, with Jane Thelwall and Kings Jester taking an individual silver medal, despite a dramatic 'no hands' moment as Jane lost her reins jumping into the Trout Hatchery, and team member Lorna Clarke scooping the bronze with her little roan horse Fearliath Mor.

A crowd of 50,000 watched on cross-country day as the British team finished miles ahead of the Netherlands, represented by husband-and-wife team

Eddy and Mandy Stibbe, and Ireland in bronze position.

Ginny's ride, Master Craftsman, was only a nine-year-old but he was a quality horse and made it all look easy. Their only near blip came in the show jumping round when a nervous Ginny nearly lost her way in the show jumping but, as she says, 'a guardian angel tapped me on the shoulder' and all was well.

Mark Phillips, whose riding career was drawing to a close, was appointed course-designer for the European championships, taking over from Philip Herbert, who is still clerk of the course at Burghley. Mark bet the ever-sporting Ian Stark, who was British team anchorman on this occasion on the hard-pulling Glenburnie and has always relished a challenge, that he would not take the direct route at a fiendishly difficult S-shaped fence, the Remy

Martin Selection, which involved three jumping efforts, all angled. No one risked it until Ian, to the disbelief of the BBC commentator, Raymond Brooks-Ward, flew straight through with a cheery wave.

RIDER OF THE DECADE

Ginny Holgate

Ginny Holgate (now Elliot) was the pin-up girl of the 1980s, a neat figure in dashing purple colours, with elfin prettiness and, like Lucinda Green, innate good manners and sparkle. She gave early notice of her talent when winning the 1973 Junior European title on Dubonnet, but a terrible fall in which she injured her arm badly was nearly career ending.

Much of her subsequent success can be attributed to her mother Heather Holgate's excellent eye for a good horse and her devoted trainer Dot Willis's attention to detail and wisdom, but it was Ginny's own mixture of bravery and accuracy that set new standards in the sport. Watching Ginny ride, one never felt it was a rehearsal – she always appeared the finished product. She was,

quite simply, a winner.

In addition to her five victories at Burghley, four of them consecutive, she also won a record three European Championship titles in a row, in 1985 (Priceless), 1987 (Night Cap ll) and 1989 (Master Craftsman), and three Badmintons, in 1985 (Priceless), 1989 (Master Craftsman) and 1993 (Welton Houdini). In some ways, the last one was the most noteworthy, as the grey Houdini had suffered a dramatic fall at Badminton in 1992 and was hunted back to confidence by Ginny over that winter.

Ginny was the first British woman to win an individual Olympic medal, bronze on Priceless at Los Angeles in 1984, and in Seoul in 1988, she added another bronze, on Master Craftsman, to the collection. In 1986, she had an outstanding winning run to land the World Championships in Gawler, Australia (on Priceless), the 'alternative' world championship in Bialy Bor, Poland, for those who could not travel so far (on Night Cap ll), and then Burghley on Murphy Himself.

The last of her 11 senior team appearances was in the 1993 European Championships at Achselschwang in

Germany and it produced one of the biggest form upsets in the sport's history when Welton Houdini, who was well in the lead after the dressage, suddenly refused at a steeplechase fence. In the face of such shocking disappointment, Ginny's beautifully executed cross-country round (she eventually finished seventh) and gracious speech to British supporters was hugely creditable, as was the sporting way in which she acknowledged the arrival of the next generation, in the shape of young Kristina Gifford who salvaged British pride with an individual silver medal.

She did, however, have the consolation a month later of her marriage to Mikey Elliot, a farmer and joint-master of the Heythrop hunt (her first marriage, to Hamish Leng, ended in divorce). Ginny's last top horse was Welton Romance, who was sold to Ireland's Lucy Thomson; they won the 1995 European title, which one senses must have been hard for Ginny to watch. By that time, she was training the British team, hunting and dabbling in point-to-point training. She later went on to be coach of the Irish eventing team in the run-up to the London Olympic Games in 2012, where they finished fifth.

Right: *Rachel Hunt (GBR), one of the leading riders of the 1980s, and Aloaf at the Remy Martin brandy glass*

The 1990s

This was the decade when eventing in Britain became truly international; Burghley only had three British winners in the 1990s. Enterprising riders from overseas were sacrificing home life and often financial security to pour into the country, mainly antipodeans, but also Belgian, French, Swedish, Dutch, Greek, Bermudan, Jamaican and German. The Americans would come over in force most autumns, and often even the smallest national event could boast competitors from about 10 different countries.

The charge had been led a decade earlier by Mark Todd and Andrew Nicholson from New Zealand, and Andrew Hoy, from Australia. By the 1990s, New Zealanders Blyth Tait, Vicky Latta, Vaughn Jefferis and Catriona McLeod were fixtures on the British circuit. Australians Matt Ryan, the 1992 Olympic champion, Clayton Fredericks, Paul Tapner and Sam Griffiths also arrived, and all found British wives.

The Kiwis, who came later than most to eventing – the first time they were represented at an international championship was in 1978 – took the sport by storm with refreshing flair and instinctive horsemanship. They dominated the 1990 and 1998 World Championships – Blyth won the individual title on both occasions, plus the 1996 Olympic title, and, Vaughan kept the world champion title in the country in 1994. The New Zealand

Left: *Open European Champion Mark Todd powers to victory on Broadcast News in 1997*

Thoroughbred, fast, brave and tough, was all the rage, and riders from all nations made annual pilgrimages in December to compete in a fun invitation competition at Puhinui, outside Auckland, and to look at horses.

Meanwhile, the swashbuckling, positive-thinking Australians thrashed the rest of the world at three successive Olympic Games, in 1992, 1996 and 2000. In the wake of a couple of fruitless Olympics, Britain was forced to examine its selection policies and team tactics, and there were several changes of personnel.

British owners took the new arrivals to their hearts and gave them horses to ride, which was sometimes a bone of contention; the media was lavish in its praise of their riding, and event organisers were only too pleased to boast an international field. Complaints were aired that British riders weren't getting a look-in and the unpopular idea of a levy on foreign riders, many of whom were by now paying British taxes and employing British grooms, was mooted and dropped.

The 1990s also saw the rise of rider power and the idea that being an event rider was a profession. Until now, competitors had rarely thought to object to cross-country fences, the state of the ground or poor prize-money, or really to question authority at all, but now horses were more valuable and the stakes higher – a dressage-judging anomaly could mean a significant difference in prize-money received.

A group of leading riders invested money into PERA (Professional Event Riders Association), which was intended as both a lobbying group and a sponsorship-raising one, but it lost impetus, partly due to the fact that riders are not always the best at organising or coordinating. The organisation has regrouped and is now named ERA (Event Riders Association) and lobbies both British Eventing and the FEI on behalf of riders.

Bill Henson was one of the first organisers to recognise that it was no longer sufficient for a top-class event to just stick up a cross-country course at the last minute, and Burghley made a major investment in irrigating the park with water from the lake and its ponds. Under Philip Herbert's management, the course was fenced off from deer and stock to keep it smooth, and great attention was paid to seeding it and managing it. This meant that even if it was a dry summer,

Far Left: The Petplan Burghley Young Event Horse was a great innovation; here is the class of 1999

there would always be a lush sward of bright green grass snaking its way around the park, a move that was unanimously appreciated by riders who could then run their horses with confidence. Burghley was always ahead of the game in the matter of horse and rider welfare.

Cross-country course design also began to change direction, partly as a direct result of the skill of the top New Zealand riders and others who could make a big track look ridiculously easy. The idea of testing rider accuracy and the horse's obedience to a greater degree with narrow or angled fences and tricky lines became more prevalent. This concept had its teething troubles and caused some commentators to bemoan the change of emphasis from the big natural-looking 'rider-frightener' fences which were more reminiscent of the hunting field and less like a showjumping test.

The idea of themed fences in novelty shapes and with adornments in the shape of animals or people also began to gain prominence, largely prompted by Irish designer Tommy Brennan's legendary Irish history-themed course at the 1991 Punchestown European championships.

There was also much debate about whether the dressage phase had become too influential, and whether 'true' eventing-type horses, in other words, the ones that were long on stamina and boldness but perhaps lacked fluidity of movement on the flat, were being penalised. Experiments with the relative influence of phases were pioneered, some the brainchild of Lucinda Green, who has long championed the cross-country phase as being the sport's crowning glory, an opinion with which most senior riders concur. Various experiments were conducted with changing or abandoning the dressage phase and one-off competitions were held.

The one that has endured is the high-octane Eventers' Grand Prix at Hickstead, a genuinely exciting challenge between eventers and showjumpers over a timed course that involves some of the Hickstead arena's famous Derby fences and a knock-down 'cross-country' course. The eventers invariably come off best.

In 1996, discussions began about Horse Trials breaking away from the British Horse Society and coming under the umbrella of the British Equestrian Federation. This was because the FEI couldn't recognise the BHS as a sporting body due to its charitable status. In 1997,

Left: *Mary King celebrates her 1996 victory with her baby daughter, Emily*

the British Horse Trials Association (now British Eventing) was formed with Michael Allen as chairman.

The calendar of events continued to expand, to more than 200, and, internationally, Pony eventing, for riders aged 13-16, gained official status during the 1990s; the first Pony European Championships were held in 1993 and the individual gold medallist was Francis Whittington, now a regular competitor at Burghley and the chairman of ERA.

A far less welcome issue during the 1990s was the necessary emphasis on risk management strategy and safer fence design. At the start of the decade, no competitor, organiser or course-designer entertained the dreadful prospect of the day ending with a rider fatality. But in 1993, a young rider, Richard Adams, was killed when his horse flipped over a table fence and landed on him at Windsor Horse Trials. He was the first of an appalling four rider deaths at national events that year.

In the next few years there were fatalities in Ireland, America, Australia and France also and, in a dreadful 12-month period from 1999 to 2000, six rider deaths in Britain, including one, Simon Long, at Burghley. The strain on everyone was evident and the sport made headlines for all the wrong reasons, being described as being more dangerous than Formula One.

Much of the criticism was unfair, for there was a great deal of soul-searching within a traumatised sport. At the end of the decade, Lord Hartington (now the Duke of Devonshire) oversaw a safety review, which led to more stringent qualifications for horses and riders and the softening of fence profiles. Although the sport remained as thrilling and as friendly as it had ever been, the reality was that eventing's truly carefree days were over as the 21st century beckoned.

1990

The Kiwis, denied a Burghley run in 1989 due to the European Championships, came back with a vengeance in this decade, none more than Mark Todd who was to dominate the headlines. At Burghley, he rode his compatriot and fellow rider Angela Davis's Face the Music, a strong ex-racehorse which, in typical Todd style, he had little acquaintance with.

They rose from 30th after dressage to second place after cross-country with the fastest round of the day. It turned out that course had been measured a minute shorter than it should have been, so no one came anywhere near the optimum time, but Mark was the fastest.

Mary Thomson was in the lead on King Cuthbert at this stage, but hit the very last show jumping fence with a sickening clunk to drop to second place behind Mark. Richard Walker's career was rejuvenated with an inspired ride on the chestnut Jacana for third place. Mary was also fourth on King Boris – her horses were always prefixed 'King' in honour of her boyfriend, David King – and the new world champion, Blyth Tait, was fifth at his first Burghley on Ricochet.

1991

Mark Todd made it two in a row, this time aboard Welton Greylag. They were second after dressage behind American rider David O'Connor, who had by now bought Mark's 1997 winner, Wilton Fair, but they had a cross-country refusal.

Welton Greylag was a classy but anxious grey horse owned and bred by Sam Barr. Sam, who was originally of Polish extraction, was one of the great characters of eventing who did much to promote British-bred horses on the world stage and was a spirited letter-writer to *Horse & Hound*. He died, aged 91 in 2011, retaining all his enthusiasm for the sport and was a regular sight on his mobile scooter.

He and his wife, Linda, ran the Welton Stud at Hartpury in Gloucestershire, and saw many of their horses – Welton Apollo, Welton Romance, Welton Crackerjack, Welton Houdini and Welton Envoy among them – go on to top honours under such good riders as Tiny Clapham, Leslie Law, Lucy Thomson, Ginny Elliot, Mark Todd and Blyth Tait.

This year, Mark Phillips had designed a daunting new Sunken Road fence at which only Carolyne Ryan-Bell and her great horse Hooray Henry, who was still competing at the age of 19, took the direct route.

Australian rider Greg Watson, who later returned home, was second on Sir Michael Turner's Chaka, a horse whose really big moment at Burghley was yet to come, and Karen Lende (now O'Connor) from America completed the international line-up in third place on Mr Maxwell, the first time no British rider had featured in the top three. Overseas riders took six out of the top 10 places, and the highest-placed British rider was Pippa Nolan (now Funnell), fourth on the little roan Sir Barnaby, one of the most popular horses on the circuit.

Tragically, Mr Maxwell and Face the Music, 10th with Mark Todd, were two of the three horses that died in the rainsoaked conditions at Badminton in 1992, a disaster which prompted greater attention to the take-offs, landings and profiles of cross-country fences.

1992

Charlotte Hollingsworth (now Bathe) and the aptly-named The Cool Customer, a superb little cross-country horse who only stood 15.3hh, were to become dependable mainstays of the British team and were part of the all-girl gold medal team at the 1994 World Equestrian Games in The Hague. Burghley, however, was easily the greatest moment of their individual career when they rose from ninth after dressage to take the lead at the end of a challenging day's cross-country and win the £10,000 first prize.

It was not the strongest Burghley field, many of the world's leading combinations being occupied with the Barcelona Olympics, but the competition was no pushover either. The weather was terrible, with torrential rain, and, typically in difficult weather conditions, it dramatically reordered the scoreboard as riders with average, or even poor, dressage marks seized the opportunity to shine across country and capitalise on the mishaps of higher-placed riders' mishaps. Pippa Funnell led the dressage phase on Metronome but retired across country. Lucinda Green was having her last ride at Burghley, on Ernie Fenwick's Up River; they were well placed after dressage and would have won but for a glance-off at Herbert's Hollow.

Blyth Tait rose from 45th place to finish second on the brilliant mare Delta, a result which helped him clinch the inaugural Land Rover World Rankings, an excellent and compulsive series which ran for most of the decade. Tim Randle, by now one of few four-star riders to have a full-time job outside eventing, as a vet, shot up from 35th to third on Legs Eleven. Kristina Gifford, one of the youngest riders in the field, gave notice of her talents with fourth on Smithstown Lad, and Brynley Powell, now a tireless organiser of the Tweseldown events, had the best four-star result of his career. He was fifth on Spiderman – he would have been second, but for showjumping faults, with the only cross-country round inside the optimum time.

On Sunday, there was an emotional moment in the main arena as Ian Stark retired his two flamboyant 'grey boys', Murphy Himself and Glenburnie, the 1991 European champion.

1993

This year saw another international line-up, and provided the biggest win of his career for the hitherto unsung American rider Stephen Bradley on the beautiful ex-racehorse Sassy Reason, his final jumping round described as 'pure class' by commentators. It was also the first USA victory for 19 years, since Stephen's mentor Bruce Davidson won on Irish Cap in 1974, and American riders took five of the top 10 places.

Mark Todd was second on Just An Ace and Andrew Nicholson was third, his best four-star result to date, riding supportive owner Rosemary Barlow's spinning Rhombus. The placing was noteworthy as Spinning Rhombus,

formerly a naughty hunter sent to Andrew to square up, was a famously reliable cross-country horse but a notoriously careless show jumper. Connections were therefore thrilled with a clear round, a dramatic improvement, turning up to prize-giving with a pink pig cuddly toy as mascot in honour of the horse's stable name, 'Piggy'.

The two top horses after dressage were withdrawn, Lucinda Murray's (now Fredericks) Just Jeremy due to bursting a blood vessel and Mary Thomson's King William because he had cut himself when shying at a pheasant. Mary had artlessly told the press about this and when they saw it published in the Saturday morning newspapers, the ground jury decided that they couldn't allow a horse with a cut, however well bandaged, to be risked across country. The only British rider in the top 10 was Frances Hay-Smith on Jabba the Hutt; Frances is now one of British Eventing's regional directors.

It was a tough Burghley that year; there were only 45 finishers from 82 starters and only 16 of them had less than 100 penalties. By now, Burghley had a permanent cross-country track which was roped off from the rest of the park and from stock. In 1993, the irrigation system which kept it lush and green was installed.

1994

By this stage, 25-year-old William Fox-Pitt had been given the ride on Chaka, the horse that was to propel him into the big time. The competition was billed as a duel between Mark Todd and Mary Thomson, but William, who had only broken into the senior ranks a few years previously, led from flagfall to win.

Chaka was a supremely talented yet enigmatic, aloof horse that had shown a tendency to slam the brakes on two-thirds of the way around the cross-country, so William had worked methodically on the horse's fitness in the run-up to Burghley, determined to put up the sort of show he knew the horse was capable of, the result being a foot-perfect performance.

Britain was back on track: Mary was second and fourth on King Kong and Star Appeal, both horses having come back from injury, and Karen Dixon was third on Too Smart. This followed in the wake of Mary and Karen's brilliant performances at the World Equestrian Games in The Hague when they were part of the all-girl British gold medal

team. However, Andrew Nicholson, seventh at Burghley on Spinning Rhombus, was the only rider to finish on his dressage score.

There was an unfortunate drama on cross-country day when Mark Todd, riding Bertie Blunt for a group of fun-loving but expectant owners new to the sport, was disqualified for missing a flag on Phase C, the second roads and tracks. By the time the information came to light Mark had gone clear round the cross-country course on Bertie Blunt. Mark was furious that officials had allowed him to go all the way round before informing him, but Bill Henson countered that 'we don't ask volunteers to be psychic'.

1995

Andrew Nicholson had by now established himself as one of the world's most indefatigable riders, known for tirelessly competing a vast variety of horses, not all of them talented. Like Blyth Tait, he had a background in preparing racehorses; he seemed to have a natural clock in his head and knew how to get a horse fit. He was also a natural horseman blessed with perfect hands and an eye for a stride, and, with a reputatio

for being able to ride anything, Andrew dominated the national rankings year after year.

He was, however, certainly not tipped to win on Buckley Province, a 13-year-old ex-racehorse that looked as delicate as porcelain. Andrew had been asked to ride the horse at Badminton the year before by previous rider Lynne Bevan, but the overseas competitor allocation was full. He told the owner, Lesley Bates, that he wasn't sure the horse would be brave enough for Burghley, but his committed cross-country riding was rewarded by his deserved first four-star win and a £12,000 first prize in Pedigree Chum's first year of sponsorship.

In another turn-up in form, Swedish rider Dag Albert, who been based in Britain for many years and was cheesed off at not being selected for the European championships that year, scored his best four-star result, in second place on Nice N Easy, a horse with feet twice the size of Buckley Province. Justine Ward scored the best result of her career in third on The Bullett.

Tina Gifford led after cross-country on General Jock but slipped to sixth place with showjumping rails down and, in another upset, Stephen Bradley, the 1993

Left: *The 1995
winner Andrew
Nicholson
celebrating with
Justine Ward, third,
and the runner-up,
Dag Albert*

winner, was eliminated for over-use of the spurs on Dr Doolittle. There were various discussions as to how the horse had come to be marked on its sides, and Steven pointed out that the marks were not in the right place for his spurs, but the ground jury felt that they had to make a stand on grounds of horse welfare. This topic had been to the fore with discussions on the use of the painkiller bute; from this year, the FEI banned the use of bute, which had previously been allowed in small doses for sore horses after cross-country.

1996

The 1996 Olympics in Atlanta was perhaps the nadir of British team fortunes and the medal-less squad and officials returned to a blizzard of criticism. One of the most bitterly disappointed was Mary King (nee Thomson), who had been in individual gold medal position when she and King William had the only cross-country fault of their career.

However, Mary whose rise in the sport owes nothing to family wealth and everything to hard work and enterprise, has a deceptively steely determination behind the ever-smiling, charming persona. Her Burghley victory in 1996 was part of a purple patch of five consecutive major wins, which included the national title at Gatcombe and Blenheim Horse Trials.

Her winning horse at Burghley, the solidly-built, Irish-bred Star Appeal, had a tendency to be headstrong and boorishly strong across country and he and Mary had had their fair share of mishaps, but by this stage they had formed a more harmonious partnership. Mary led the dressage phase with Bruce Davidson, but he had a cross-country fall, leaving her in the lead. In the following week, the papers and magazines were full of pictures of the Pedigree Chum trophy being clasped by a smiling baby Emily King.

Second place went to Andrew Nicholson, who was again masterful on a less than clean jumper, Cartoon, a handsome bay horse he had taken over from Pippa Funnell. Matt Ryan was third on an ex-racehorse, Hinnegar, and Pippa Funnell had a breakthrough fourth place on the bouncy skewbald Bits and Pieces. Vicky Latta, who was to return to New Zealand and her law career, made her last four-star appearance, in 18th place on Home Run.

Left: *Mary King and Star Appeal en route to victory in 1996*

1997

As part of a short-lived FEI experiment, the European Championships of 1997 were declared 'open', so that riders outside Europe, many of whom were based in the northern hemisphere anyway, could compete in them and gain Olympic qualifications, and in a complicated move, two sets of medals were awarded.

Burghley was chosen to host it and, as Mark Phillips was by now training the American team, it was not appropriate for him to design the cross-country course, so that honour went to Mike Tucker, a former rider and prominent BBC commentator, who proved an imaginative and creative deputy.

The level of the course was technically reduced to three-star standard, in line with European championship status, but it was no pushover with a relentless onslaught of combination fences and a picturesque new route through the water which involved going under the Lion Bridge followed by a galloping stretch against the beautiful backdrop of Burghley House shimmering in the early autumn sunshine.

The course proved hugely influential, and there were several falls, with a couple of riders hospitalised. Four of the top six riders after the dressage phase fell – David O'Connor, who was to become the 2000 Olympic champion, Pia Pantsu, a dashing Finnish rider, Lucy Thompson, the reigning European champion, and Chris Bartle, who won Badminton the following year.

Bettina Overesch (now Hoy), had done a customarily brilliant dressage test on the grey Watermill Stream, but she incurred time penalties on the steeplechase, so that left Mark Todd in the lead after having what he later described as the ride of a lifetime on Broadcast News, a little black New Zealand Thoroughbred produced by his team mate Vicky Latta.

The next day, there was all sorts of controversy at the final horse inspection. Watermill Stream and Cosmopolitan, lying third with William Fox-Pitt, both appeared unsound and were sent to the holding box for re-inspection, although to loud cheers from the crowd, both horses were passed at the second attempt. However, a horse ridden by Phillip Dutton was failed, which eliminated the Australian team, and this caused ill feelings in some areas.

Andrew Nicholson's horse, Dawdle, was withdrawn, a factor which helped the British team to win the gold medal convincingly, but it was Mark Todd's day, an equally popular result, and jubilant scenes abounded with his two young children, Lauren and James, wearing his medals to the press conference.

Bettina became European champion, the crowning moment of her career, and William Fox-Pitt won his first senior individual medals, Open European bronze and European silver. Kristina Gifford (now Cook) scored her best Burghley result with a European bronze medal on General Jock.

1998

The reigning Olympic champion Blyth Tait equalled Mark Todd's record of a one-two, riding Chesterfield and Aspyring, in a year of mud and mayhem. The competition got off to a controversial start when Blyth vociferously objected to his dressage mark of 55 on Chesterfield and threatened to withdraw, but event director Bill Henson took it calmly, joking that all publicity is good publicity, and the situation was diffused.

In the event, the dressage became largely irrelevant because the rain poured down and the ground conditions deteriorated dramatically. Andrew Nicholson was again brilliant and finished third on Hinnegar, despite being virtually last after dressage.

Only 23 out of the field of 63 completed the competition, with notable scalps including Pippa Funnell on Supreme Rock, Mark Todd with the ex-racehorse Stunning, and the dressage leaders Paddy Muir and Archie Brown among the retirements. No one came anywhere near the optimum cross-country time, several accrued time penalties on a boggy steeplechase track and only four horses were clear in the showjumping, Chesterfield, who won easily, among them.

Jancis Tulloch, whose husband Andrew is now clerk of the course at Aintree, was the best British rider in fourth place on Bally Free. Another notable performance was that of New Zealander Dan Jocelyn on the eight-year-old Silence, who made a meteoric rise to sixth.

This Burghley was part of an extraordinarily successful period for Blyth, a hugely competitive rider who added great wit, colour and cheer during his 15 years at the top of the British eventing scene. That summer, he had won the British Open at Gatcombe, and a month after Burghley he achieved his second world title, spearheading a virtual New Zealand whitewash at the World Equestrian Games in Pratoni del Vivaro, Italy.

Burghley 1998 also marked the launch of the Rolex Grand Slam, in which Rolex offered a $250,000 bonus (now $350,000) to the rider who could win Burghley, Badminton and Kentucky, in any order, in a 12-month period. It was an irresistible challenge, but one which riders deemed impossible, so difficult is it to bring a horse to four-star level, let alone win. Blyth did indeed set off for Kentucky the following spring to try his luck, but he finished second.

1999

This was a year of great drama also, but for all the wrong reasons. On the Friday of Burghley, several eventing personnel decamped to the nearby funeral of Polly Phillipps, who had been killed in a fall at Thirlestane Castle in Scotland. She should have been competing at Burghley that afternoon.

The following day, the shock and sadness was amplified when Simon Long, a cheerful rider who loved his hunting and team chasing and epitomised old-fashioned eventing spirit, died in a fall at the new Sunken Water fence at his first Burghley. His horse, Springleaze Macaroo, ground to a halt at the rail on the way out of the complex and, in his enthusiasm, Simon made the fateful decision to turn the horse right and ask him to jump the alternative rail. The horse chested the rail, flipped over and landed on Simon.

At a reception that evening to mark the Horse Trials Support Group's 21st anniversary, the Princess Royal made a moving speech to try to boost a thoroughly dispirited group of people. 'Horses do not always share our aspirations," she said.

Blyth Tait suffered a fall at the same fence as Simon, although with far less tragic consequences, and was taken to hospital with a broken leg. Although an investigation found no fault with the fence design – Mark Todd deemed it a perfectly fair question - Mark Phillips was asked to 'tone down' his course in future.

There were a record 24 first-timers

in the field of 75, of which only 37 completed the competition. Eighteen retired or were eliminated on the cross-country and nine horses were withdrawn overnight.

The winner, Mark Todd, who made the course look deceptively easy on both his winning horse, Diamond Hall Red, and Word for Word, third, had by this stage announced his retirement from the sport would be in 2000. It was his 25th three-day event win and his fifth at Burghley, equalling Ginny Elliot's record, and it came with a typical Todd twist.

His two horses' places were actually reversed before the showjumping phase: he was in the lead on the quality New Zealand Thoroughbred Word For Word, second at Badminton that year, and was lying third on the jumping-bred Diamond Hall Red, who few spectators had heard of before. The bright chestnut, owned by farmer's wife Pat Smith, was notoriously difficult on the flat but had been sent eventing after demonstrating his jumping prowess in the hunting field.

However, Mark jumped clear on Diamond Hall Red and then hit four show jumps on Word For Word so the placings were reversed. Karen Dixon was second – she finished on the same score as Mark but he was faster across country, so prevailed – on Too Smart, the brilliant successor to her great Olympic campaigner Get Smart. It turned out to be Karen's best ever four-star result for, like Ian Stark, she was destined to be a top-flight rider who never won Burghley.

RIDER OF THE CENTURY

Mark Todd

Mark Todd, perhaps the most extraordinary natural horseman the sport has ever seen, was named Rider of the Century by the FEI in 2000, the year of his 'retirement'. When he was born in 1956, the sport was virtually unknown in New Zealand and his enthusiasm for it was entirely fired by books about horses and by his grandfather, Pop, a dairy farmer who bought him a pony. Mark grew up as an all-round horseman, doing more show jumping than eventing, and dabbling in racing.

He was a member of New Zealand's first ever eventing team, at the disastrous World Championships of 1978 in Kentucky, for which he had to fund his own trip, but it only served to make him keener to try his fortune on the world stage. He travelled to England in 1979 – Andrew Nicholson was on the same plane – and, with Andrew as his groom, won Badminton in 1980 as a first-timer, on Southern Comfort. This was a record that was to stand for more than 30 years.

In 1983, he sold his dairy herd and became united with the horse with whom he will forever be associated: Charisma, a little black gelding, mainly thoroughbred but with a tiny drop of Percheron blood, whose personality matched his talent. They won numerous international competitions, were second at Burghley and second twice at Badminton and they put New Zealand eventing on the map when they won back-to-back Olympic titles in 1984 in Los Angeles and 1988 in Seoul (plus a team bronze at the latter). This was the first time a rider had achieved this since Dutchman Lt Charles Ferdinand Pahud de Morganges in 1928 and 1932 on Marcroix.

During the 1990s, Mark was part of the silver medal Kiwi team at the Barcelona Olympics, although his horse, Welton Greylag, went lame, and he missed the Atlanta Olympics due to horse injury. However, he was still the pre-eminent rider of the decade, winning numerous other competitions, four Burghleys and two Badmintons, in 1994 and 1996, and making a name for his magical ability to form instant partnerships with horses after only the briefest of acquaintances. His Badminton victory in 1994 was a case in point, as he had never sat on the horse, Lynne Bevan's Horton Point, before the competition and he was drawn first to go.

The Kiwis dominated the 1990 and 1998 World Equestrian Games, and Mark added a world individual silver in 1998 on Broadcast News, the nearest he has got to a world title, to the Open European gold the year before at Burghley.

Mark made Britain his home in the 1990s, with wife Carolyn and their children Lauren and James. In 2000, after he won an individual bronze medal on Eye Spy at the Sydney Olympics, the family flew home to New Zealand to start a new life with racehorses. It wasn't long before he had trained a Classic winner, Bramble Rose in the New Zealand Oaks.

The next part of the story is part of sporting legend. Mark was at a dinner party in 2007 with eventing friends when it was lightly suggested he made a comeback in time for the 2008 Beijing Olympics (for which the equestrian sports would be in Hong Kong). This involved qualifying from scratch in just eight months. Amazingly, this was achieved, on a horse called Gandalf, and after only eight international competitions, Mark found himself drawn not only first for the team in Hong Kong, but first in the entire competition. He finished 18th individually and decided to return to England for a second eventing career.

At the 2010 World Equestrian Games in Kentucky (he was the only rider to have competed in the 1978 version as well), he was part of New Zealand's first team medal, bronze, for 10 years. In 2011, in a remarkable sporting achievement, he won Badminton for the fourth time, on NZB Land Vision (31 years after his first victory); in 2012, aged 56, he rode in his sixth Olympic Games and won a team bronze medal on NZB Campino. Also in 2012, Mark began the next chapter in his riding life by buying a farm and stables in Wiltshire, and he was appointed trainer to the Brazilian team for the 2016 Rio Olympics. In recognition of his contribution to eventing, he was knighted in the New Year Honours of 2013.

2$1^{st}$ Century Burghley

The most dramatic development in eventing in the 21st century was the shortening of the format so that the roads and tracks and steeplechase phases were dropped. The move horrified purists, some of whom still mourn the loss of the military-style preparation and camaraderie which accompanied those earlier cross-country days, but it is a development which, in hindsight, is seen to have had some benefits.

The decision was prompted by the necessity to shorten the competition at the 2004 Olympics in Athens where only very limited space was available. This proved a propitious move, because in 2002 the sport of eventing was earmarked as one that should be dropped

from the Olympic movement, although this was avoided.

Since then, other championships, including the 2006 World Equestrian Games in Aachen, Germany, and the 2008 Olympic competition in Hong Kong, have been held in constricted areas. It was also felt that the traditional style of eventing was too onerous and expensive for many organisers, especially in countries where space, funding and expertise were limited. Burghley held out until 2005, after which Phases A, B and C were abandoned.

The chief worries were that horses would no longer be produced for stamina – and, indeed, the fashion for buying flashy-moving Continental warmbloods

Left: *The former Olympic champion Matt Ryan inspects the cross-country course with designer Mark Phillips - here they are on the edge of the Leaf Pit*

did take over for a while – and that younger riders, no longer traditionally reared in the hunting field, would lose all sense of the importance of judging pace and getting a horse fit.

It is probably fair to say that, in some quarters, those skills may have deteriorated, but as riders grappled with the idea of setting off across country 'in cold blood' without the warming-up phases realisation dawned that horses still needed to be thoroughly fit and the Thoroughbred horse has regained ground at the top of the sport. Another benefit is that horses are doing less mileage, which means they are, in general, able to stay in the sport for longer and do more competitions. Although those with a longer history look back with nostalgia on the epic cross-country days of the past, many riders admit that they don't miss the heroics involved at all.

Far from diminishing the sport's appeal to spectators, many of whom were completely oblivious to what was going on in the preliminaries to cross-country, and to riders, Burghley's attendance and status has continued to grow under director Elizabeth (Liz) Inman. In tandem with the sport's more modern look, she became, in 2005, the first woman to direct a four-star event in Britain. Liz had a long apprenticeship in the things that mattered when working as assistant to Bill Henson, and she has since governed with a steady grace and charm that has kept Burghley right at the top of the sport and as popular as ever.

2000

The first Burghley of the new millennium was a colourful one. The winner of the £20,000 first prize was Andrew Nicholson on Mr Smiffy, a tearaway chestnut who had unnerved several other riders before finding mutual respect with the New Zealander. Andrew himself nearly fell off at the Waterloo Rails – one photographer managed to capture him apparently performing a handstand on the horse's shoulders.

Most leading riders had set off for the Sydney Olympics, but Mark Todd decided to risk one last run on British soil at his favourite event, and he finished eighth on Just A Mission, saying: 'I must be mad.' It was an emotional weekend for him, bidding farewell to a community which had taken him to their hearts over 20 years, and there were tears all round when he paraded an aged but perky

Far Left: *Liz Inman & former chairman Malcolm Wallace*

Charisma in the main arena on Sunday.

The real headline-snatching performance was that of Vere Phillipps, on his late wife Polly's horse, Coral Cove. A well-known dealer and a respected horseman in the hunting field and showjumping ring, he had set himself the task of qualifying from scratch in one season to ride Coral Cove at Burghley in Polly's memory. This seemed a near-impossible task, and one tabloid heading screamed: 'Novice risks danger ride', but, amazingly, everything went according to plan, perhaps aided by one of Vere's clients paying £500 for him to have dressage lessons 'to save embarrassment'.

At Burghley, Vere rose from 20th after dressage to finish eventual fourth and win the prize for best Burghley debut, telling people that when he went cross-country he would imagine a fox had got up behind the start box. Everywhere he went, he was followed by deafening cheers from the crowd; the press lapped up his amusing quotes and didn't miss the story that he was beginning a romance with the third-placed rider, Clea Hoeg-Mudd (they are now married). 'I feel I've given it my best shot,' he said. 'Eventing is a great sport, it's been a great year and

a real tonic. I just wish Polly had been here to see this.'

At the request of the FEI, Mark Phillips had made the cross-country markedly softer than it had been in 1999; there were 38 clear rounds from the 68 starters.

2001

This year was the closest Burghley came to not taking place. Foot-and-mouth disease had decimated the eventing season, which didn't really get going until July, and major events Badminton, Chatsworth and Gatcombe were all cancelled. The risk was subsiding by September, but the problem was the impossibility of insuring the event against cancellation. Thanks to the sponsor, Pedigree, and Bill Henson, who refused to be beaten, the event went ahead, with a record entry of 108. It was underwritten by 37 'Friends of Burghley' who generously pledged £10,000 each. Mike Tucker took over designing the course this year, and had to work to a strict budget.

It was also decided that Burghley should test the new Olympic format proposed for Athens 2004 of two showjumping rounds. The IOC felt that riders should not be able to get two medals, team and individual, for one riding performance; the compromise was that the top 25 riders would jump again to decide the individual medals.

Therefore, amid a certain amount of consternation, riders at Burghley jumped twice, and this played into the hands of the eventual winner, Blyth Tait, who excelled in this phase and jumped two clear rounds to score a fifth successive New Zealand victory at Burghley. Andrew Nicholson very nearly achieved a record back-to-back win on Mr Smiffy, but had one fence down in the first jumping round to be second. In a Kiwi whitewash, Dan Jocelyn was third on Silence.

Blyth's winning mount, Ready Teddy, was one of the great event horses of the era and hugely popular. He was a cheerful, white-faced chestnut New Zealand thoroughbred, an ex-racehorse. Blyth took him as an eight-year-old to the Atlanta Olympics as a reserve; he ended up getting a run, jumped out of his skin and won the individual Olympic gold medal. The pair went on to win numerous competitions, including the 1998 world title.

2002

Bill Henson engaged the German maestro Wolfgang Feld to design Burghley's cross-country course. Wolfgang, who was 67 by then, had been famously associated with Luhmuhlen, Germany's premier event, for 24 years, had been designing for 37 years, and had produced the acclaimed cross-country course at the Barcelona Olympics. He was well known to be a strong character, and there was much interest in how things would go at Burghley.

Considerable investment was put into re-working the layout of the site. Mark Phillips had had the big drop at the Leaf Pit as an early fence; Wolfgang had it approached in a reverse (uphill) direction, and he also reversed the direction of the course so that the arena fences came early. For the first time, spectators were banned from walking on the course to preserve the going; by now, more irrigation pipes had been laid across the estate and about £100,000 had been spent on providing perfect footing.

Wolfgang's course proved, as anticipated, highly influential and 52 out of the field of 95 completed, with 36 clear rounds from those who finished the

competition. William Fox-Pitt found himself a surprised winner on Carole Hudson's nine-year-old Highland Lad, a horse that was unruly in the dressage phase but a brilliant jumper.

Andrew Nicholson led after cross-country, but a sixth consecutive New Zealand win was thwarted when his horse, New York, was lame at the final inspection. Instead, there was a British one-two-three, with Polly Stockton dropping to second with a fence down on Word for Word, the ride she had taken over from Mark Todd, and Mary King third on King Solomon. 'Not a Kiwi in sight,' William couldn't resist saying to the press.

2003

Bill Henson couldn't have wished for a more exciting finale in his last year as director of Burghley. By this stage Zara Phillips, whose parents, Princess Anne and Capt Mark Phillips, had both won Burghley before, was competing at the top level, on Toytown, her young rider horse. Burghley was to be her four star debut, and there was feverish media excitement, something Zara has always taken with sanguine good grace.

Above: *Liz Inman with ground jury members Jane Tolley and Jean Mitchell*

The other thriller on the horizon was that in the spring Pippa Funnell had won Kentucky and Badminton, the first two legs of the Rolex Grand Slam worth $250,000 to the rider who can capture those two events and Burghley in the same 12 months. This represented riches beyond any event rider's ken, and the pressure was nearly too much for Pippa, who arrived at Burghley in a state of high tension.

Unbelievably, by Sunday morning, Pippa, riding Denise and Roger Lincoln's leggy, elegant Primmore's Pride, a winner of the Burghley Young Event Horse final a few years previously, and Zara were tied on the same score after cross-country. Zara, however, had the upper hand because she had finished faster across country on the bold Toytown and nearer the optimum time than Pippa, whose horse had a tendency

Above: *I did it: Pippa Funnell, holding aloft her Rolex watch and a cheque for $250,000, achieves the seemingly impossible*

to dwell in the air over fences.

As Pippa cleared the final showjumping fence, she broke into a wide smile, knowing that she had done her best and could do no more except wait and see. The crowd was on the edge of their seats, but as Zara and Toytown hit the penultimate fence, they let out a great groan, which signalled to Pippa, waiting in isolation in the collecting ring, that she had won the biggest prize in eventing history.

Zara was incredibly sporting in defeat but her great moments – the European title in 2005 and the world title in 2006 – were yet to come and, as Bill Henson had remarked that morning, if he had to choose between the two riders, he felt that Zara, the younger, still had plenty of time for a big win.

Pippa's story was to inspire generations of young riders. She enjoyed great success as a junior and young rider on her distinctive roan horse, Si

Left: *Pippa Funnell on her way to an epic win on Primmore's Pride*

Right: *Vintage performance: 25 years after his first victory, Andrew Hoy wins Burghley again, on Moonfleet*

LITTLE BOOK OF **BURGHLEY**

Barnaby, but senior recognition was harder to come by and, after a succession of high-profile failures at four-star level, Pippa sought help from the modern phenomenon of sport psychology.

Her Rolex Grand Slam and Burghley victory were part of a golden period for Pippa which included three Badminton wins, three Olympic medals and back-to-back European titles. Married to the showjumper William Funnell, she is now heavily involved in their successful Billy Stud enterprise but is still riding at four-star level and pleasing the crowds.

2004

The 2004 running marked a briefly unhappy period in Burghley's history, a dreadful baptism by fire for the young Andrew Tulloch, who temporarily succeeded Bill Henson as event director, and a tragic end to Wolfgang Feld's distinguished course-designing career.

The weather was hot and sticky and the ground on the steeplechase course had become dull and tiring. Riders voiced their unhappiness about this, plus a couple of fences on the cross-country course, and requested that the steeplechase be shortened. However, the ground jury and technical delegate decided against it.

There was, therefore, something of a febrile atmosphere on cross-country morning. Later in the afternoon, Caroline Pratt, a quiet but accomplished horsewoman, was killed when her horse Primitive Streak hit a jetty fence at the Lion Bridge near the end of the course, rotated over it and landed on her in the water. The accident was watched by horrified riders on close-circuit television and a photographer made himself unpopular by sending the pictures to a newspaper, which published them on the front page next day.

There was an outpouring of grief among competitors, and Carl Bouckaert, the rider representative on the FEI Eventing Committee, jumped on a plane from his home in the States to try and ameliorate the situation, as everyone assembled, red-eyed, in the main arena for a minute's silence for Caroline. One consequence of the incident is that moves were made to tighten procedures concerning rider representation and there was also the creation of an ad-hoc committee who would mediate in the case of controversy.

Amid all this drama, the victory of Andrew Hoy, who rode brilliantly on the classy Irish thoroughbred Moonfleet, was somewhat overlooked. This was unfortunate, for it was a terrific sporting achievement for him to win Burghley again 25 years after the first time in 1979. The sport had changed so much, in terms of technical difficulty, that the ability of riders like Andrew, Mark Todd, Andrew Nicholson and Mary King to maintain their game over decades cannot be underestimated. Andrew Hoy had famously won three consecutive Olympic team gold medals for Australia, but four-star success had eluded him for a quarter-century.

2005

Liz Inman, for so many years Bill Henson's right-hand woman, was promoted to event director, the first female to run a four-star in Britain. Happily for her, her appointment coincided with the arrival of Land Rover, one of the most stalwart backers of the sport and of Burghley over many years, as title sponsor.

Mark Phillips was back as course-designer for what was to be Burghley's last long-format three-day event with steeplechase and roads and tracks phases. William Fox-Pitt was the rider to enter the history books as the last winner of a British four-star in this style. He led throughout on Ballincoola, a wonderfully genuine Irish-bred chestnut owned by one of his most loyal supporters, Judy Skinner, a driving force behind the Event Horse Owners Association which aims to ensure better conditions for owners at events.

2006

The Rolex Grand Slam loomed large over Burghley again in 2006, and this time Andrew Hoy was in the hot seat, having won Kentucky on Master Monarch and Badminton for the first time, on Moonfleet. He came agonisingly close to matching Pippa Funnell's achievement three years previously when he led the first two phases, but a sickening clatter of poles in the final phase signalled an end to the dream and he finished second – so near and yet so far.

Australia's national anthem still rang out, but it was for Lucinda Fredericks

who by this stage had taken the nationality of her husband, Clayton. Andrew showed remarkable grace as Lucinda took centre stage for her win on one of the most popular horses of the decade, Headley Britannia. It was an Australian whitewash, as Shane Rose finished third on All Luck.

For Lucinda, one of the bubbliest riders around, this was a big moment and, with a first prize cheque of £45,000, a lucrative one, for over the years she had sold many good horses in order to survive financially. She was also disappointed to have been left off the Australian team at the World Equestrian Games in Aachen.

'Brit', who stood just 15.2hh but had a big, generous heart and jumped as if on springs, was only the second mare to win in Burghley's history, following Maid Marion 33 years earlier. The story was made even better by the fact that she had nearly died from a virus the previous year, and that she was a horse Lucinda had tried, and failed, to sell. In 2007, Lucinda and Headley Britannia joined the elite group of partnerships to capture Burghley and Badminton in the same 12 months, and two years later they won Kentucky.

2007

Continuity was assured at Burghley when Miranda Rock, the granddaughter of Burghley's founder, succeeded her mother, Lady Victoria Leatham, as president of the horse trials.

It was also business as usual for William Fox-Pitt who won Burghley again – it was his seventh three-day event win of 2007. This time his winning mount was Philip Adkins' Parkmore Ed, a classy horse but one that had not had the best of preparations for Burghley.

By this stage, Mark Phillips was well into his stride at Burghley and produced a course which he described as 'the biggest in the world this year'. It was certainly a track for the most experienced, and at the end of cross-country day, only Andrew Nicholson on Lord Killinghurst stood between William and Burghley win number four. Lord Killinghurst, a hugely consistent four-star horse, was not, however, the best of showjumpers, and when he faulted, victory was William's.

2008

This was another occasion when the very experienced riders came to the fore. Burghley was beset by unusually terrible weather, so much so that Liz Inman and her team had to hold their nerve to run at all on cross-country day and by the end of the weekend everything and everyone was covered in thick mud.

'MW' Guinness had been disappointed that her beloved horse, Tamarillo, was not selected for the British team with William Fox-Pitt for the Olympic three-day event, held in Hong Kong in August, but it all worked out for the best. Tamarillo, a horse William had at first discounted as a potential eventing star, had grown into arguably the best cross-country horse of his generation. A light-boned part Arab, part Polish thoroughbred bred by Finn Guinness, he was perfectly equipped to skip through the quagmire on cross-country day – he had won Badminton in similar conditions in 2004 - and he gave William one of the most exhilarating rides of his career.

It was Tamarillo's one and only run at Burghley – he was usually in demand for team championships at this stage of the season – and, because it was new to him, he concentrated and didn't spook. Tamarillo and Barry's Best, ridden by

Rosie Thomas, were the only horses to finish inside the optimum time of 11 minutes 30 seconds.

The first and second-placed riders after dressage, Ruth Edge and Lucy Wiegersma, both retired on the cross-country, and there were 10 falls, including one for Zara Phillips. William was left with two fences in hand on the final day over American rider Phillip Dutton, but he withdrew his horse, Woodburn, on the final morning.

Thus William finished first and second – the third rider to do so after Mark Todd and Blyth Tait – on Tamarillo and Ballincoola, and his long-time team mate and friend Mary King was third and fourth on Imperial Cavalier and Apache Sauce.

2009

After so many 'senior' winners at Burghley, Oliver Townend was an exciting new talent on the winner's rostrum. A blunt and amusing Yorkshireman, Oliver had been trained by Ken Clawson, jumping trainer to the British team, and had become highly competitive on the domestic circuit. He had won Badminton in the spring,

on Flint Curtis, and followed this up with a convincing win at Burghley on another grey, Carousel Quest, an elegant horse produced by Cressie Clague-Reading who had previously been fourth at Burghley on the horse. Rolex Grand Slam fever set in once more after this, but Oliver's quest for the big bonus came to a painful end with a nasty fall at Kentucky in the following spring, which just shows how thin the line between success and failure can be when a horse is involved.

2010

Caroline Powell, who originally came to Britain to work as a groom for Ian Stark, made history as the first New Zealand female rider to win a four-star when she triumphed on the popular grey Lenamore who, at 17 years old, was the oldest equine Burghley winner and, at 15.3hh, probably the smallest. Caroline, a modest but highly effective horsewoman, was also the first winner based north of the border since Lorna Clarke in 1978.

Due to the event's proximity to the World Equestrian Games in Kentucky, one-third of the field were first-timers.

but they didn't really get a look in. William Fox-Pitt was second and sixth, Clayton Fredericks third, Oliver Townend fourth, and 49-year-old Mary King was fifth and seventh and the only rider to have two horses round clear inside the time. And Mark Todd reappeared at Burghley, 10 years after his last visit, as if he'd never been away and finished 11th on Major Milestone.

2011

Amid emotional scenes, William Fox-Pitt rode into the record books with his sixth Burghley win, putting him ahead of two heroes of eventing, Ginny Elliot and Mark Todd, an accolade he says means more to him than any of his other achievements. 'I pretend to look relaxed, but deep down this really matters to me,' he said. His winning mount was Parklane Hawk, a New Zealand Thoroughbred and as quality a stamp of event horse as any, owned by Catherine Witt.

Andrew Nicholson was second on long-time owner Libby Sellar's Nereo, a horse bred in Spain, illustrating the point that brilliant event horses can still come from a multitude of origins. Mary

King was a popular third on her home-bred mare Kings Temptress, a result which contributed to her becoming the first woman since Pippa Funnell to be world number one and the first to win the HSBC FEI Classics, a lucrative series which linked the world's six four-star events.

2012

Burghley visibly benefited from the 'Olympic bounce', as crowds poured in wanting another fix of the thrilling, high-octane action they'd watched during the London Olympic Games and to have a second chance to see a couple of the Olympic fences jumped in a Burghley setting. And while everyone agreed the 'pop-up' cross-country day in the tight confines of Greenwich Park had been the pinnacle of an incredible fortnight of equestrian sport, Burghley's meaty track, where the only real way to go was all the direct routes, was still the real deal to which all event riders aspire.

A last-minute drenching made the ground holding and influential and only four riders were inside the

optimum time, with the boldest riders making meteoric rises up the scoreboard in time-honoured, old-fashioned eventing style.

In contrast to his two earlier wins, this time Andrew Nicholson was tipped to win this time, a reflection of the increasing quality of his string of horses. His third Burghley victory, for a £55,000 cheque, came aboard one he bred himself, the crowd-pleasing grey, Avebury. The result was also a popular triumph for Avebury's owner, Rosemary Barlow, who has helped raise more than £1 million for Britain's teams but had been waiting 35 years to win a four-star event as an owner.

William Fox-Pitt was third on Parklane Hawk and collected his third HSBC FEI Classics title, worth $150,000, by just one point in the tightest finish yet to the series.

A few new faces made it into the upper echelons, notably the graceful US rider Sinead Halpin in second place, talented young Kiwi Jock Paget in fifth, and Izzy Taylor, great-niece of Burghley's first winner, Anneli-Drummond Hay, in a perfect example of how the wheel keeps turning in eventing.

Left: Andrew Nicholson clocks up a third Burghley win in Olympic year, on long-time owners Rosemary and Mark Barlow's delightful grey Avebury

BURGHLEY TODAY

The secret of Burghley's success is continuity: through the riders themselves, who are driven to return year after year because it still represents the ultimate achievement, the spectators for whom it is an unmissable annual pilgrimage, and the officials and volunteers, many of whom are former competitors, not to mention the long-standing sponsor, Land Rover, and legions of tradestand-holders.

Capt Mark Phillips, the course-designer, first rode at Burghley in the 1960s; Philip Herbert, clerk of the course, worked with the original architect of the cross-country course at Burghley, Bill Thompson, and designed the tracks for championships in the 1980s; Liz Inman, the director, was brought up in the environs of the park at Burghley, is steeped in the local hunting and point-to-pointing scene, and first came to work in the horse trials office, as a secretary, in 1979. Her right-hand women, Jacqueline Stevens, who manages the tradestands, and competition secretary Anne Whitton, have been involved for some 30 years. And none of it would have been possible without the foresight and generosity in 1961 of the sports-loving Marquess of Exeter, whose granddaughter, Miranda Rock, now fronts the world's best-loved horse trials in her ancestors' beautiful parkland. Long may it last.

RIDER OF THE DECADE

William Fox-Pitt

William Fox-Pitt, who was born in 1969, is officially the most successful event rider of all time, having notched up his 50th international win in 2012, at Blenheim on Seacookie. Born into an eventing family – his parents, Marietta and Oliver, both competed – he has won medals at all levels for Great Britain, starting at Junior level when his contemporaries included Pippa Funnell and Kristina Cook. The 2012 London Olympics, his fourth Games, was his 15th senior cap and his 17th senior medal.

Educated, articulate and approachable, William was the first British rider to be world number one in eventing and in 2008 he was the inaugural winner of the HSBC Classics.

William's first major win was at Burghley on Chaka in 1994 when he was 25; in 2011, he beat the joint record of five wins set by Ginny Elliot and Mark Todd when he scored his sixth victory, aboard Parklane Hawk.

On leaving university, where he read French, William set up in business in Oxfordshire with his then girlfriend, later wife, Wiggy Channer (she is now the partner of Andrew Nicholson). There were many triumphs, but also some rocky times and it was only latterly that William became so dominant in the sport with such a high-quality string of

Right: *Six of the best: William Fox-Pitt rides into the record books with a sixth Burghley win, on Parklane Hawk*

horses and an assured yet sympathetic riding style which, for many people, marks him out as perhaps the best horseman of the early 21st century.

The horse with whom he will always be associated is Tamarillo, a spooky and contrary but supremely talented part Arab who, at first sight, looked an unlikely superstar. They won Badminton in 2004 and might have won Olympic gold in 2004 at Athens had Tamarillo not chipped a bone in his knee during the cross-country, which was a cruel blow. However, the partnership recovered and went on to win European team gold and individual silver medals in 2005, team silver at the World Equestrian Games in Aachen in 2006, and Burghley in 2008.

William also won European team gold medals in 1995, 1997, 2001, 2003 and 2009. In 2010, he led the British team to gold at the World Equestrian Games in Kentucky and collected the individual silver medal on Cool Mountain.

In 2004, he married *Channel Four Racing* presenter Alice Plunkett, the only woman to have completed Badminton and the Aintree course. They live on a family estate in Dorset with a menagerie of animals and have three young children, Oliver, Thomas and Chloe.

Roll of Honour

- 1961 Anneli Drummond-Hay/Merely-a-Monarch/GBR

- 1962 Capt James Templar/M'Lord Connolly/GBR [European Champion]
  Team: USSR

- 1963 Harry Freeman-Jackson/St Finbarr/IRL

- 1964 Richard Meade/Barberry/GBR

- 1965 Capt Jeremy Beale/Victoria Bridge/GBR

- 1966 Capt Carlos Moratorio/Chalan/ARG [World Champion]
  Team: Ireland

- 1967 Lorna Sutherland/Popadom/GBR

- 1968 Sheila Willcox/Fair and Square/GBR

- 1969 Gillian Watson/Shaitan/GBR

- 1970 Judy Bradwell/Don Camillo/GBR

- 1971 HRH Princess Anne/Doublet/GBR [European Champion]
  Team: Great Britain

- 1972 Janet Hodgson/Larkspur/GBR

- 1973 Capt Mark Phillips/Maid Marion/GBR

- 1974 Bruce Davidson/Irish Cap/ USA [World Champion]
  Team: USA

- 1975 Aly Pattinson/Carawich/GBR

- 1976 Jane Holderness-Roddam/ Warrior [GBR]

- 1977 Lucinda Prior-Palmer/George/ GBR [European Champion]
  Team: Great Britain

- 1978 Lorna Clark (neé Sutherland]/ Greco (GBR)

- Junior European Champion: Dietrich Baumgart/Kurfurst/West Germany
  Team: West Germany

- 1979 Andrew Hoy/Davey/AUS

- 1980 Richard Walker/John of Gaunt/GBR

- 1981 Lucinda Prior-Palmer/Beagle Bay/GBR

- 1982 Richard Walker/Ryan's Cross/ GBR

Left: *Princess Anne and Doublet, who remains her most remembered horse, fly across country en route to victory at Burghley in 1971*

Far Right:
Caroline Powell riding the diminutive grey Lenamore to victory in 2010

- 1983 Virginia Holgate/Priceless/GBR

- Jean-Paul Saint Vignes/Jocelyn A/FRA [Young Rider European Champion]
  Team: Great Britain

- 1984 Virginia Holgate/Night Cap ll/GBR

- 1985 Virginia Holgate/Priceless [European Champion]

- 1986 Virginia Leng (neé Holgate)/Murphy Himself (GBR)

- 1987 Mark Todd/Wilton Fair/NZL (also second on Charisma)

- 1988 Jane Thelwall/King's Jester/GBR

- 1989 Virginia Leng/Master Craftsman/GBR [European Champion]
  Team: Great Britain

- 1990 Mark Todd/Face The Music/NZL

- 1991 Mark Todd/Welton Greylag/NZL

- 1992 Charlotte Hollingsworth/The Cool Customer/GBR

- 1993 Stephen Bradley/Sassy Reason/USA

- 1994 William Fox-Pitt/Chaka/GBR

- 1995 Andrew Nicholson/Buckley Province/NZL

- 1996 Mary King/Star Appeal

- 1997 Mark Todd/Broadcast News/NZL [Open European Champion]

- Bettina Overesch/Watermill Stream/GER [European Champion]
  Team: Great Britain

- 1998 Blyth Tait/Chesterfield/NZL (also second on Aspyring)

- 1999 Mark Todd/Diamond Hall Red/NZL

- 2000 Andrew Nicholson/Mr Smiffy/NZL

- 2001 Blyth Tait/Ready Teddy/NZL

- 2002 William Fox-Pitt/Highland Lad/GBR

- 2003 Pippa Funnell/Primmore's Pride/GBR [Rolex Grand Slam winner]

- 2004 Andrew Hoy/Moonfleet/AUS

- 2005 William Fox-Pitt/Ballincoola/GBR

- 2006 Lucinda Fredericks/Headley Britannia/AUS

- 2007 William Fox-Pitt/Parkmore Ed/GBR

- 2008 William Fox-Pitt/Tamarillo/GBR
  (also second on Ballincoola)

- 2009 Oliver Townend/Carousel Quest

- 2010 Caroline Powell/Lenamore/NZL

- 2011 William Fox-Pitt/Parklane Hawk/GBR

- 2012 Andrew Nicholson/Avebury/NZL

The pictures in this book were provided courtesy of the following:

KIT HOUGHTON
WWW.HOUGHTONSHORSES.COM

HORSE & HOUND PICTURE ARCHIVES

Design and artwork by Scott Giarnese

Published by G2 Entertainment Limited

Publisher: Jules Gammond

Written by Kate Green